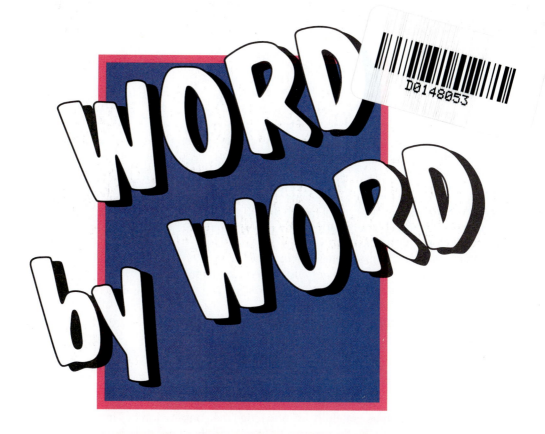

WORD by WORD

Literacy Workbook

Steven J. Molinsky · Bill Bliss

Contributing Authors
Dorothy Almanza
Deborah L. Schaffer
Carol H. Van Duzer

Longman

Publisher: *Mary Jane Peluso*
AVP / Director of Production and Manufacturing: *Aliza Greenblatt*
Executive Managing Editor: *Dominick Mosco*
Electronic Production and Page Composition: *Wendy Wolf*
Electronic Production Specialists: *Carey Davies and Steven Greydanus*
Art Director / Cover Design: *Merle Krumper*
Interior Design: *Kenny Beck and Wendy Wolf*
Manufacturing Manager: *Ray Keating*
Pre-formatter: *Rose Ann Merrey*

Illustrations: *Richard E. Hill*

The authors gratefully acknowledge the contribution of Tina Carver
in the development of the *Word by Word* program.

© 1999 by PRENTICE HALL REGENTS
Pearson Education
10 Bank St., White Plains, NY 10606

All rights reserved. No part of this book may be
reproduced, in any form or by any means,
without permission in writing from the publisher.

Printed in the United States of America

10   9   8   7   6

ISBN 0-13-150939-X

CONTENTS

A. CIRCLE THE SAME WORD

1. NAME	STREET	NUMBER	(NAME)	STATE
2. CITY	STATE	ADDRESS	CITY	LAST
3. ADDRESS	ADDRESS	NAME	NUMBER	CITY
4. STATE	STREET	FIRST	LAST	STATE
5. STREET	FIRST	STATE	STREET	LAST

B. MATCHING

1. STATE   MAIN STREET

2. ZIP CODE   045-61-8947

3. STREET   NANCY PETERSON

4. TELEPHONE NUMBER   CA

5. NAME   684-1196

6. SOCIAL SECURITY NUMBER   22960

ABCDEFGHIJKLMNOPQR

C. FILL OUT THE FORM

NAME: _____
           FIRST   LAST

ADDRESS: _____
           NUMBER   STREET   APT.

_____
           CITY   STATE   ZIP CODE

TELEPHONE NUMBER: _____

SOCIAL SECURITY NUMBER: _____

D. FILL OUT THE FORM

NAME
    FIRST   LAST

ADDRESS
    NUMBER   STREET   APT.

    CITY   STATE   ZIP CODE

TELEPHONE NUMBER

SOCIAL SECURITY NUMBER

STUVWXYZ 0123456789

E. INTERVIEW

Talk to three people. Write the information.

Name	Telephone Number
1. _____	_____
2. _____	_____
3. _____	_____

F. LISTENING

Listen and circle the words you hear.

1. (name)
   address

2. zip code
   apartment number

3. telephone
   social security

4. state
   street

5. middle
   city

6. first
   last

G. JOURNAL

My first name is _____.

My last name is _____.

My address is _____.

My telephone number is _____.

A. WHO ARE THEY?

1.	grandmother	<u>b</u>
2.	son	___
3.	father	___
4.	daughter	___
5.	mother	___
6.	grandfather	___

B. MATCHING

1.	FATHER	sister
2.	SISTER	mother
3.	BROTHER	daughter
4.	MOTHER	father
5.	SON	brother
6.	DAUGHTER	son

Aa Bb Cc Dd Ee Ff Gg Hh Ii Jj Kk Ll Mm

C. WHAT'S MISSING?

1. w_i_fe

   s_ster

2. fathe_

   mothe_

3. hu_band

   _on

4. grands_n

   br_ther

5. b_by

   d_ughter

6. grandmo_ _er

   grandfa_ _er

D. WHICH GROUP?

daughter	father	son	wife
husband	brother	sister	mother

Parents

Children

1. f a t h e r

2. m _ _ _ _ _

3. h _ _ _ _ _

4. w _ _ _

5. s _ _

6. d _ _ _ _ _ _ _

7. b _ _ _ _ _

8. s _ _ _ _ _

Nn Oo Pp Qq Rr Ss Tt Uu Vv Ww Xx Yy Zz

FAMILY MEMBERS II

A. WHO ARE THEY?

1. nephew   <u>d</u>

2. aunt   ____

3. niece   ____

4. cousin   ____

5. uncle   ____

B. WHAT'S MISSING?

1. a <u>u</u> n t

   _ n c l e

2. _ e p h e w

   _ i e c e

3. c _ _ u s i n

   s _ n – i n – l a w

4. s i s t _ _ – i n – l a w

   b _ o t h _ _ – i n – l a w

C. WHICH GROUP?

aunt	cousin	nephew	niece	uncle

<u>n e p h e w</u>   c _ _ _ _ _   a _ _ _

<u>u</u> _ _ _ _   n _ _ _ _

D. WHO ARE THEY?

aunt	uncle

1. He's my _____<u>uncle</u>_____ .

2. She's my _____ .

father	aunt

5. He's my _____ .

6. She's my _____ .

nephew	niece

3. He's my _____ .

4. She's my _____ .

sister	uncle

7. He's my _____ .

8. She's my _____ .

E. JOURNAL

This is my family.

My _____ 's name is _____ .

My _____ 's name is _____ .

My _____ 's name is _____ .

A. THE COMPASS

Write each word on the correct line.

north	south	east	west

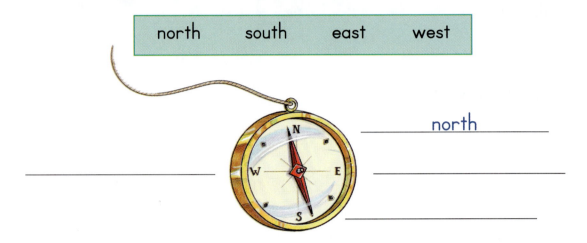

north

B. WHERE IS IT?

north	south	east	west

1. Canada is <u>n o r t h</u> of the United States.

2. Mexico is <u>s</u> _ _ _ _ of the United States.

3. California is <u>w</u> _ _ _ of Utah.

4. Texas is _ _ _ _ of Arizona

5. Florida is _ _ _ _ _ of New York.

C. LISTENING

Listen and circle the word you hear.

1. (north)   south   4. west   east

2. east   west   5. south   north

3. north   south   6. east   west

A. WHICH CONTINENT?

Bolivia	Brazil	Germany	Peru	Poland	Spain

South America

B r a z i l

P _ _ _

B _ _ _ _ _ _

Europe

P _ _ _ _ _

S _ _ _ _

G _ _ _ _ _ _

China	Japan	Korea	Morocco	Somalia	Sudan

Africa

S _ _ _ _

S _ _ _ _ _ _

M _ _ _ _ _ _

Asia

K _ _ _ _

J _ _ _ _

C _ _ _ _

B. JOURNAL

My name is _____.

I am from _____.

Now I live in _____.

A. MATCHING

1.    take a bath

2.    brush my teeth

3.    comb my hair

4.    get up

5.    take a shower

6.    go to bed

B. WHAT DO YOU DO EVERY DAY?

brush	eat	make	shave	sleep	wash

1. I ____make____ breakfast.

2. I _____ my hair.

3. I _____ my face.

4. I _____ dinner.

5. I _____ .

6. I _____ .

C. LISTENING

Listen. Write the correct number.

___ take a shower   ___ make dinner

___ brush teeth   ___ shave

_1_ take a bath

11

A. LISTENING

Listen. Put a check under the correct picture.

1.   ✓   2.

3.   4.

5.   6.

B. MATCHING

1. wash   TV

2. play   the dishes

3. watch   the cat

4. feed   basketball

C. WHAT DO YOU DO EVERY DAY?

| dust | study | vacuum | play | watch TV | exercise |

1. I _____study_____ . 2. I _____ . 3. I _____ .

4. I _____ . 5. I _____ . 6. I _____ .

D. LISTENING

Listen. Write the correct number.

___ sweep   ___ wash the dishes

___ vacuum   ___ do the laundry

_1_ exercise   ___ play basketball

E. JOURNAL

Every day I _____ , I _____ ,

I _____ , and I _____ .

A. WHAT'S THE WORD?

teacher	student	board	desk	book
pencil	clock	ruler	notebook	map

a. _____ clock _____   f. _____

b. _____   g. _____

c. _____   h. _____

d. _____   i. _____

e. _____   j. _____

B. LISTENING

Listen and circle the word you hear.

1. pen   (pencil)   4. eraser   ruler

2. pencil   paper   5. notebook   textbook

3. chalk   clock   6. computer   calculator

C. WHAT'S IN THE CLASSROOM?

Look at page 10 of the dictionary. Write the correct word.

| map | book | clock | computer | globe |

1. There's a c l o c k next to the flag.

2. There's a g _ _ _ _ on the bookshelf.

3. There's a b _ _ _ on the teacher's desk.

4. There's a m _ _ next to the bulletin board.

5. There's a _ _ _ _ _ _ _ _ next to the TV.

D. JOURNAL

In my classroom there is _____

_____

_____.

A. LISTENING

Listen. Put a check under the correct picture.

1. ____✓____   _____

2. _____   _____

3. _____   _____

4. _____   _____

5. _____   _____

6. _____   _____

B. MATCHING

1. Stand   your name.

2. Write   down.

3. Open   up.

4. Sit   your book.

C. WHAT'S THE ACTION?

Close	Go	Turn off	Work
Do	Raise	Watch	Write

1. _____Write_____ your name.

2. _____ to the board.

3. _____ your book.

4. _____ the movie.

5. _____ your hand.

6. _____ your homework.

7. _____ the lights.

8. _____ in groups.

COUNTRIES, NATIONALITIES, AND LANGUAGES

A. MATCHING

Country	Nationality	Language
1. Mexico	Chinese	Amharic
2. China	Cambodian	Spanish
3. Haiti	Ethiopian	Chinese
4. Cambodia	Mexican	Haitian Kreyol
5. Ethiopia	Haitian	Cambodian

B. LISTENING

Listen and circle the country you hear.

1. Japan	(Thailand)		4. Spain	Estonia
2. Russia	Costa Rica		5. Canada	Cambodia
3. Poland	Portugal		6. Ecuador	El Salvador

C. JOURNAL

My name is _____.

I am from _____.

My nationality is _____.

I speak _____.

A. CHOOSE THE CORRECT ANSWER

1. a. She lives in a house.
   b. She lives in an apartment.

2. a. He lives in a dormitory.
   b. He lives in a cabin.

3. a. They live in a trailer.
   b. They live in a houseboat.

4. a. She lives in a nursing home.
   b. She lives in a farmhouse.

B. WHAT TYPE OF HOUSING?

1. c a b i n

2. t _ _ _ _ _ _

3. h _ _ _ _

4. f _ _ _ _ _ _ _

5. a _ _ _ _ _ _ _ _

6. s _ _ _ _ _ _

A. CIRCLE THE CORRECT WORD

1. sofa
   (armchair)

2. coffee table
   bookcase

3. rug
   pillow

4. lamp
   plant

5. floor
   wall

6. painting
   window

B. WHERE IS IT?

Look at page 14 of the dictionary. Write the correct word.

1. There's a l a m p on the end table.

2. There's a p _ _ _ _ _ _ _ on the bookcase.

3. There are d _ _ _ _ _ _ on the window.

4. There's a p _ _ _ _ _ _ _ _ on the wall.

5. There's a p _ _ _ _ _ on the sofa.

C. WHAT'S THE WORD?

bookcase	lamp	plant	sofa	window
fireplace	pillow	rug	television	

1. _____sofa_____   2. _____   3. _____

4. _____   5. _____   6. _____

7. _____   8. _____   9. _____

D. JOURNAL

In my living room there is _____

_____.

THE DINING ROOM

A. WHAT'S IN THE DINING ROOM?

1. c a n d l e

2. t _ _ _ _ _

3. c _ _ _ _ _

4. p _ _ _ _ _ _

5. t _ _ _ _ _

B. MATCHING

1. china   bowl

2. salt   dish

3. butter   shaker

4. salad   pot

5. coffee   cabinet

C. LISTENING

Listen and circle the words you hear.

1. (butter dish)   salt shaker   4. table   tablecloth

2. teapot   pitcher   5. teapot   coffee pot

3. salt shaker   pepper shaker   6. creamer   sugar bowl

A. CHOOSE THE CORRECT ANSWER

1. (a.) The cup goes on the saucer.
   b. The saucer goes on the cup.

2. a. The napkin goes on the fork.
   b. The fork goes on the napkin.

3. a. The knife goes to the right of the teaspoon.
   b. The teaspoon goes to the right of the knife.

4. a. The soup spoon goes to the right of the teaspoon.
   b. The soup spoon goes to the left of the teaspoon.

B. WHAT IS IT?

1. g l a s s

2. c _ _

3. n _ _ _ _ _ _

4. t _ _ _ _ _ _ _ _

5. k _ _ _ _

6. f _ _ _

A. WHAT'S THE WORD?

| bed | blanket | blinds | dresser | mirror | pillow |

1. _____pillow_____   2. _____   3. _____

  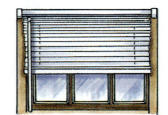

4. _____   5. _____   6. _____

B. MATCHING

1. night   radio
2. alarm   spring
3. jewelry   clock
4. twin   table
5. clock   box
6. box   bed

C. WHERE IS IT?

Look at page 17 of the dictionary. Write the correct word.

1. The alarm clock is on the <u>n i g h t s t a n d</u>.

2. The pillow is on the _ _ _.

3. The jewelry box is on the _ _ _ _ _ _ _.

4. The _ _ _ _ _ is between the bed and the bureau.

5. The _ _ _ _ _ _ is over the dresser.

6. The _ _ _ _ _ _ are on the window.

D. LISTENING

Listen and circle the words you hear.

1. (blanket)
   blinds

2. mattress
   dresser

3. bedspread
   box spring

4. dresses
   mirror

5. pillow
   blanket

6. alarm clock
   clock radio

E. JOURNAL

In my bedroom there is _____

_____

_____.

A. WHAT'S IN THE KITCHEN?

cabinet	oven	sponge	dishwasher	refrigerator
stove	sink	toaster	microwave	

1. _dishwasher_

2. _____

3. _____

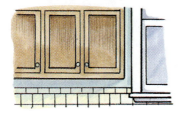

4. _____

5. _____

6. _____

7. _____

8. _____

9. _____

B. WHICH GROUP?

dishwasher	microwave	range	sink

For cooking:

_____ microwave _____

_____

For cleaning:

_____

_____

A. WHAT IS IT?

1. g r a t e r

2. p _ _

3. w _ _

4. b _ _ _ _ _ _ _

5. l _ _ _ _

6. s _ _ _ _ _ _ _

B. MATCHING

1. pie   kettle

2. tea   maker

3. popcorn   plate

4. can   pan

5. roasting   opener

C. LISTENING

Listen. Write the correct number.

___ mixer   ___ frying pan

___ tea kettle   ___ can opener

_1_ blender   ___ popcorn maker

A. WHAT IS IT?

car seat   doll   stroller   crib   high chair   swing

1. _____stroller_____

2. _____

3. _____

4. _____

5. _____

6. _____

B. MATCHING

Look at page 20 of the dictionary. Complete the sentences.

1. The doll is   in the crib.

2. The baby is   on the changing table.

3. The intercom is   in the playpen.

4. The stuffed animal is   in the toy chest.

5. The stretch suit is   on the chest.

28

A. WHAT IS IT?

1. <u>o i n t m e n t</u>

2. <u>b</u> _ _ _ _ _ _

3. <u>n</u> _ _ _ _ _ _

4. <u>b</u> _ _

5. <u>p</u> _ _ _ _ _ _ _ _

6. <u>b</u> _ _ _   _ _ _ _

B. MATCHING

1. baby   swabs

2. diaper   powder

3. teething   ring

4. cotton   diapers

5. disposable   pins

C. LISTENING

Listen. Write the number under the correct picture.

_ _   l   _ _   _ _   _ _

A. WHAT'S IN THE BATHROOM?

| bath mat | mirror | shower | soap | toothbrush |
| bathtub | plunger | sink | toilet | |

1. _____plunger_____

2. _____

3. _____

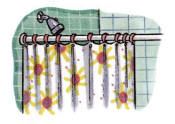

4. _____

5. _____

6. _____

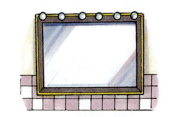

7. _____

8. _____

9. _____

B. LISTENING

Listen and circle the word you hear.

1. mat   (mirror)   4. toilet   towel

2. sink   scale   5. plunger   sponge

3. shelf   shower   6. cup   tub

PERSONAL CARE PRODUCTS

A. WHAT IS IT?

1. <u>c o m b</u>

2. r _ _ _ _

3. _ _ _ _ _ _ _ _ _ _ _

4. _ _ _ _ _ _ _

5. _ _ _ _ _ _ _ _

6. _ _ _ _   _ _ _ _ _

B. WHICH GROUP?

brush	conditioner	mouthwash	toothbrush
comb	dental floss	shampoo	toothpaste

For teeth

dental floss

_____

_____

_____

For hair

_____

_____

_____

_____

C. LISTENING

Listen. Write the correct number.

____ comb   ____ scissors   ____ shampoo

____ powder   1 hair brush   ____ toothpaste

A. WHAT IS IT?

1. <u>b r o o m</u>

2. <u>m</u> _ _

3. <u>d</u> _ _ _ _ _ _ _

4. _ _ _ _

5. _ _ _ _ _ _ _

6. _ _ _ _ _ _

B. MATCHING

Look at page 24 of the dictionary. Complete the sentences.

1. The washer is   on the dryer.

2. The broom is   next to the dryer.

3. The trash can is   on the clothesline.

4. The clothespins are   next to the dustpan.

5. The laundry detergent is   next to the utility sink.

C. LISTENING

Listen and circle the words you hear.

1. (bleach)   broom   4. cleanser   cleaner

2. dryer   iron   5. bucket   pail

3. dry mop   sponge mop   6. sponge   starch

A. WHAT IS IT?

| chimney | lamppost | mailbox | garage | lawnmower | window |

1. _____mailbox_____

2. _____

3. _____

4. _____

5. _____

6. _____

B. MATCHING

1. doorknob   garage

2. letter   lawnmower

3. television   door

4. grass   mailbox

5. car   TV antenna

THE APARTMENT BUILDING

A. CHOOSE THE CORRECT WORD

1. smoke detector
   (fire alarm)

2. buzzer
   peephole

3. intercom
   elevator

4. balcony
   lobby

5. garbage chute
   laundry room

6. parking lot
   parking garage

B. MATCHING

1. laundry   conditioner

2. swimming   lot

3. parking   room

4. smoke   chute

5. garbage   pool

6. air   detector

A. WHO IS IT?

| carpenter | electrician | gardener | locksmith | painter | plumber |

1. ___locksmith___   2. _____   3. _____

4. _____   5. _____   6. _____

B. MATCHING: WHO REPAIRS IT?

1.   television   plumber

2.   sink   locksmith

3.   steps   electrician

4.  light   carpenter

5.   door lock   TV repair person

A. WHAT IS IT?

1. <u>s a w</u>

2. <u>h</u> _ _ _ _ _

3. <u>p</u> _ _ _ _ _

4. <u>w</u> _ _ _ _ _

5. <u>d</u> _ _ _ _

6. <u>s</u> _ _ _ _ _ _ _ _ _ _

B. MATCHING

1. drill   nail

2. screwdriver   bit

3. hammer   brush

4. nut   screw

5. paint   bolt

C. LISTENING

Listen. Write the correct number.

___ hammer   ___ sandpaper

___ saw   _1_ electric drill

___ scraper   ___ power saw

GARDENING TOOLS AND HOME SUPPLIES

A. WHAT IS IT?

flashlight   mousetrap   rake
hose   plunger   shovel

1. _____plunger_____   2. _____   3. _____

4. _____   5. _____   6. _____

B. MATCHING

1. garden   seeds

2. hedge   cord

3. vegetable   hose

4. fly   measure

5. tape   swatter

6. extension   clippers

A. MATCHING

1. five   5

2. three   7

3. six   8

4. eight   3

5. seven   6

B. WHAT'S THE NUMBER?

1. nine   _____9_____

2. three   _____

3. sixteen   _____

4. twelve   _____

5. seventy   _____

C. WHAT'S THE WORD?

4   _____four_____

6   _____

13   _____

40   _____

100   _____

D. LISTENING

Listen and circle the number you hear.

1. (13)   30   3. 17   70   5. 42   24

2. 14   40   4. 16   60   6. 35   53

E. MATCHING

1. third   9th
2. ninth   60th
3. first   12th
4. twelfth   3rd
5. sixtieth   1st

6. eleventh   80th
7. eighth   11th
8. fourth   14th
9. eightieth   4th
10. fourteenth 8th

F. WHAT'S THE NUMBER?

1. second   ___2nd___
2. tenth   _____
3. thirteenth _____
4. first   _____
5. fiftieth   _____
6. third   _____

G. WHAT'S THE WORD?

14th   ___fourteenth___

6th   _____

60th   _____

11th   _____

20th   _____

21st   _____

H. MATCHING

1. four   fifth
2. five   second
3. two   fourth
4. one   third
5. three   tenth
6. ten   first

I. LISTENING

Listen and circle the number you hear.

1. 4th   (14th)   40th
2. 7th   17th   70th
3. 3rd   13th   30th
4. 8th   18th   80th
5. 2nd   22nd   32nd

A. MATCHING

1. 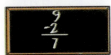 3X2=6

2. 8÷2=4

3. $\frac{9}{-2}$ $\frac{}{7}$

4. $\frac{+4}{5}$

subtraction

addition

multiplication

division

B. MATCHING

1. minus   x

2. times   +

3. equals   −

4. plus   ÷

5. divided by   =

C. LISTENING

Listen and circle the answer.

1. +   −   ⊗   ÷

2. +   −   x   ÷

3. +   −   x   ÷

4. +   −   x   ÷

5. +   −   x   ÷

D. WRITE THE MATH PROBLEMS

1. One plus three equals four.

$$\frac{\begin{array}{r}1\\+3\end{array}}{4}$$

2. Eight divided by four is two.

3. Two times five equals ten.

4. Twelve minus seven is five.

E. WHAT'S THE FRACTION?

1/4   _____   _____   _____   _____

F. MATCHING

1. one half   2/3

2. one quarter   3/4

3. two thirds   1/2

4. three fourths   1/3

5. one third   1/4

G. LISTENING

Listen and circle the answer.

1. (1/3)   1/4

2. 1/4   1/2

3. 1/4   3/4

4. 1/4   3/4

5. 1/2   2/3

H. WHAT'S THE PERCENT?

75%   _____   _____   _____

I. MATCHING

1. fifty percent   25%

2. twenty-five percent   50%

3. one hundred percent   30%

4. thirty percent   75%

5. seventy-five percent   100%

J. LISTENING

Listen and write the percent you hear.

1.   50%   4. _____

2. _____   5. _____

3. _____   6. _____

A. WHAT TIME IS IT?

8:00

_____

_____

_____

_____

_____

_____

_____

B. CHOOSE THE CORRECT ANSWER

1. a. It's a quarter to four.
   b. It's a quarter to three.

2. a. It's seven thirty.
   b. It's six thirty.

3. a. It's five thirty.
   b. It's six twenty-five.

4. a. It's a quarter to five.
   b. It's a quarter after five.

C. MATCHING

1.	a quarter to four	4:30	ten to five
2.	four twenty	4:15	three forty-five
3.	half past four	3:45	four thirty
4.	a quarter after four	4:50	twenty after four
5.	four fifty	4:20	four fifteen

D. CHOOSE THE CORRECT TIME

1. (7:00 A.M.)
   7:00 P.M.

2. noon
   midnight

3. noon
   midnight

4. 10:00 A.M.
   10:00 P.M.

E. LISTENING

Listen and circle the time you hear.

1. 2:30   (8:30)   4. 5:45   6:45

2. 10:00   2:00   5. 1:30   2:30

3. 3:15   4:15   6. 5:01   1:05

F. JOURNAL: MY DAILY SCHEDULE

I get up at _____. I eat breakfast at _____.

I go to school at _____. I have lunch at _____.

I eat dinner at _____. I go to sleep at _____.

A. WHAT'S MISSING?

1. J a _n_ u a r y
2. F _ b r u a r y
3. M a _ c h
4. A _ _ i l
5. M _ _
6. J _ _ e
7. J _ _ y
8. A _ g _ _ t
9. S _ _ t _ _ b e r
10. O _ _ o _ e r
11. N _ _ _ _ _ _ _
12. D _ _ _ _ _ _ _

B. WRITE THE MONTH

1. January _February_ March
2. March April _____
3. June _____ August
4. August _____ October
5. October November _____

C. WHAT'S MISSING?

1. S _u_ n d a y
2. M o _ d a y
3. T u e _ d _ _
4. W e _ n e s _ _ _
5. T h _ _ _ d a y
6. F _ _ _ _ _ _
7. S _ _ _ _ _ _ _

D. WRITE THE DAY

1. Sun. _____Sunday_____

2. Mon. _____

3. Tue. _____

4. Wed. _____

5. Thur. _____

6. Fri. _____

7. Sat. _____

E. MATCHING

1. 7/10/98   March 6, 1997

2. 5/8/99   January 2, 1999

3. 1/2/99   February 1, 1999

4. 2/1/99   July 10, 1998

5. 3/6/97   May 8, 1999

F. WRITING

1. What day is it?   It's _____.

2. What year is it?   It's _____.

3. What month is it?   It's _____.

4. What's today's date?   Today is _____.

G. LISTENING

Listen and circle the correct answer.

1. (Monday)   Sunday

2. Thursday   Tuesday

3. June   July

4. November   December

5. April 4   April 14

6. May 7   March 7

45

A. WHAT'S THE PLACE?

bank	hospital	hair salon	coffee shop
clinic	drug store	gas station	grocery store
bakery	book store	bus station	hardware store

1. _____clinic_____

2. _____

3. _____

4. _____

5. _____

6. _____

7. _____

8. _____

9. _____

10. _____

11. _____

12. _____

B. MATCHING

1. flower shop   pharmacy

2. gas station   day-care center

3. drug store   service station

4. auto dealer   florist

5. child-care center   car dealer

C. MATCHING

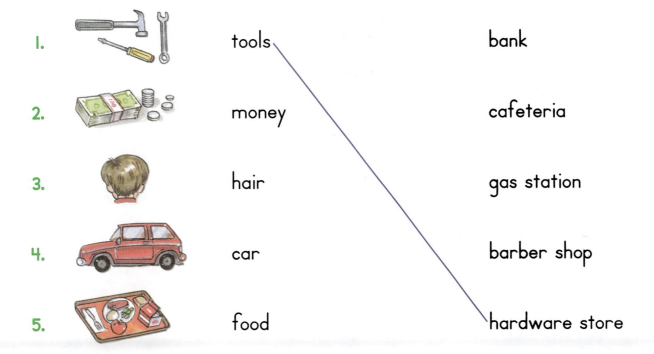

1. tools   bank

2. money   cafeteria

3. hair   gas station

4. car   barber shop

5. food   hardware store

D. LISTENING

Listen and circle the place you hear.

1. barber shop
   (coffee shop)

2. book store
   drug store

3. clothing store
   hardware store

4. appliance store
   discount store

5. copy center
   concert hall

6. bus station
   gas station

PLACES AROUND TOWN II

A. WHAT'S THE PLACE?

mall	garage	library	supermarket
park	museum	laundromat	parking lot
hotel	school	restaurant	post office

1. _____museum_____

2. _____

3. _____

4. _____

5. _____

6. _____

7. _____

8. _____

9. _____

10. _____

11. _____

12. _____

B. MATCHING

1.  book — parking lot

2.  letter — library

3.  teacher — school

4.  dinner — post office

5.  car — restaurant

C. WORDSEARCH

```
H R Z O O L V Q S L Y M Z T
T Y C F N Z I L K I M A D E
Q S L P A R K B C B Q L T D
P C F N C Y L P U R G L C E
S H J S U P E R M A R K E T
S O R Q Y A O J G R V D W C
V O C K H O T E L Y N B R U
R L Q T B S I A M D P H L Z
B O L A U N D R O M A T F X
```

___ HOTEL   ___ MALL   ✓ SUPERMARKET

___ PARK   ___ ZOO   ___ LAUNDROMAT

✓ LIBRARY   ___ SCHOOL

A. WHAT'S THE WORD?

bus	bus stop	parking meter	pedestrian
taxi	street sign	traffic light	meter maid
sewer	sidewalk	taxi driver	police officer

1. _____meter maid_____

3. _____

2. _____

4. _____

5. _____

7. _____

6. _____

8. _____

11. _____

9. _____

12. _____

10. _____

50

B. MATCHING

1. police   light

2. parking   booth

3. phone   station

4. traffic   container

5. trash   meter

C. WHICH GROUP?

| bus driver | intersection | police officer | taxi driver |
| bus stop | pedestrian | police station | taxi stand |

People

bus driver

_____

_____

_____

Places

_____

_____

_____

_____

D. YES OR NO?

Look at pages 38–39 of the dictionary. Answer <u>Yes</u> or <u>No</u>.

<u>No</u> 1. The police officer is on the sidewalk.

_____ 2. The police officer is in the intersection.

_____ 3. The fire station is next to the courthouse.

_____ 4. The police station is next to the courthouse.

_____ 5. The bus is in front of a taxi.

A. WHAT'S THE WORD?

clean	dirty	full	new	open	small
closed	empty	large	old	short	tall

1. _____new_____   3. _____   5. _____

2. _____   4. _____   6. _____

7. _____   9. _____   11. _____

8. _____   10. _____   12. _____

B. MATCHING: OPPOSITES

1. fast   low
2. big   light
3. heavy   tight
4. high   little
5. loose   slow

6. wide   light
7. old   narrow
8. good   cold
9. dark   bad
10. hot   young

C. WHAT'S THE WORD?

| cold | dull | heavy | narrow | plain | short | single |

1. Is his hair long?

   No. It's <u>s h o r t</u>.

2. Is she married?

   No. She's _ _ _ _ _ _ _.

3. Is the street wide?

   No. It's _ _ _ _ _ _.

4. Is the water hot?

   No. It's _ _ _ _.

5. Is the dress fancy?

   No. It's _ _ _ _ _.

6. Is the box light?

   No. It's _ _ _ _ _.

7. Is the knife sharp?

   No. It's _ _ _ _.

A. LISTENING

Listen. Put a check under the correct picture.

1. _____ ✓_____ 2. _____ _____

3. _____ _____ 4. _____ _____

5. _____ _____ 6. _____ _____

7. _____ _____ 8. _____ _____

9. _____ _____ 10. _____ _____

B. CHOOSE THE CORRECT WORD

1. shocked
   (proud)

2. happy
   afraid

3. tired
   pleased

4. upset
   exhausted

5. annoyed
   ashamed

6. jealous
   nervous

C. WHICH GROUP?

ecstatic	miserable	pleased	proud	unhappy	upset

"happy" words

_____ecstatic_____

_____

_____

"sad" words

_____

_____

_____

D. JOURNAL

I feel _____ today

because _____

_____ .

A. WHAT'S THE WORD?

| apple | grapes | lime | peach | plum |
| banana | lemon | orange | pear | |

1. ____lemon____ 2. _____ 3. _____

4. _____ 5. _____ 6. _____

7. _____ 8. _____ 9. _____

B. LISTENING

Listen and circle the fruit you hear.

1. (cherries)   cranberries   4. banana   papaya

2. limes   lemons   5. grapes   dates

3. plums   prunes   6. tangerine   nectarine

VEGETABLES

A. WHAT'S THE WORD?

1. <u>o n i o n</u>

2. t _ _ _ _ _

3. c _ _ _ _ _

4. _ _ _ _ _ _ _

5. _ _ _ _ _ _

6. _ _ _ _ _ _ _

7. _ _ _ _

8. _ _ _ _ _ _

9. _ _ _ _ _ _ _

B. MATCHING

1. acorn   potato

2. red   bean

3. sweet   squash

4. lima   sprout

5. brussels   pepper

57

A. WHAT'S THE WORD?

butter	cheese	eggs	orange juice	soda	spaghetti
cereal	cookies	milk	rice	soup	yogurt

1. _____milk_____

2. _____

3. _____

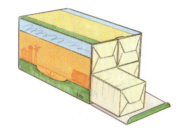

4. _____

5. _____

6. _____

7. _____

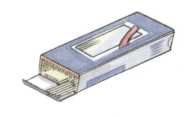

8. _____

9. _____

10. _____

11. _____

12. _____

B. WHAT'S THE WORD?

1. r o l l s

2. c _ _ _ _ _ _ _

3. s _ _ _ _ _

4. _ _ _ _ _ _

5. _ _ _ _ _

6. _ _ _   _ _ _ _ _

C. WHICH GROUP?

ham	pork	shrimp	margarine
duck	trout	crackers	tuna fish
soup	turkey	macaroni	sour cream

Dairy Products

margarine
_____

_____

Canned Goods

_____

_____

Packaged Goods

_____

_____

Meat

_____

_____

Poultry

_____

_____

Seafood

_____

_____

A. CHOOSE THE CORRECT WORD

1. ketchup
(mustard)

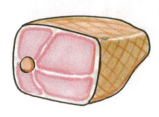

2. ham
jam

3. salt
pepper

4. olives
olive oil

5. tissues
napkins

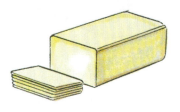

6. mozzarella
mayonnaise

7. soap
soup

8. coupon
popcorn

9. peanuts
pretzels

10. coffee
cashier

11. plastic bag
paper bag

12. scale
scanner

B. MATCHING

1.	Swiss	sauce		6.	roast	oil
2.	soy	towels		7.	potato	beef
3.	salad	cheese		8.	cooking	food
4.	cake	dressing		9.	trash	chips
5.	paper	mix		10.	dog	bags

C. WHICH GROUP?

flour	napkins	pickles	roast beef	sugar	trash bags
ketchup	peanuts	potato chips	soap	tissues	turkey

Deli

turkey

_____

Snack Foods

_____

_____

Condiments

_____

_____

Baking Products

_____

_____

Paper Products

_____

_____

Household Items

_____

_____

D. JOURNAL

What do you need from the supermarket?

My Shopping List

_____ _____

_____ _____

A. WHAT'S THE WORD?

bag	bottle	bunch	dozen	head	loaf	pound
bar	box	can	gallon	jar	pint	quart

 1. a <u>dozen</u> eggs

 8. a _____ of butter

 2. a _____ of soup

 9. a _____ of bread

 3. a _____ of flour

 10. a _____ of soap

 4. a _____ of jam

 11. a _____ of milk

 5. a _____ of lettuce

 12. a _____ of ice cream

 6. a _____ of carrots

 13. a _____ of milk

 7. a _____ of crackers

 14. a _____ of soda

B. MATCHING

1. a jar of   soda

2. a box of   eggs

3. a liter of   tuna fish

4. a bunch of   cereal

5. a can of   jelly

6. a dozen   paper towels

7. a roll of   bananas

C. WORDSEARCH

```
L  S  A  P  Q  M  W  R  V  G  Q  N  B  S
S  C  B  E  O  Y  J  L  O  A  F  B  D  D
O  A  R  S  B  Q  J  A  B  L  O  K  O  C
A  N  E  F  P  I  N  T  V  L  D  J  B  B
R  I  H  R  S  Q  D  S  N  O  L  A  D  S
B  R  Q  O  X  Z  N  I  F  N  E  R  V  B
U  B  O  T  T  L  E  B  M  X  P  A  S  T
Q  A  O  L  A  R  J  Z  L  D  O  Z  E  N
A  G  M  P  O  U  N  D  O  N  B  U  E  Y
```

___ BAG   ___ DOZEN   ___ PINT

___ BOTTLE   ___ JAR   ___ POUND

___ CAN   ✓ LOAF   ✓ GALLON

A. MATCHING

1. Tbsp.   ounce

2. pt.   gallon

3. gal.   tablespoon

4. lb.   fluid ounce

5. oz.   pound

6. tsp.   pint

7. fl. oz.   teaspoon

B. WHAT'S THE NUMBER?

1. 1 cup = __8__ fl. ozs.

2. 1 gal. = ___ fl. ozs.

3. 16 fl. ozs. = ___ pt.

4. 1 lb. = ___ ozs.

5. 1 qt. = ___ fl. ozs.

C. LISTENING

Listen and circle the amount you hear.

1. (ounce)   gallon   4. 8 lbs.   8 ozs.

2. Tbsp.   tsp.   5. 1/4 lb.   3/4 lb.

3. lb.   oz.   6. cup   quart

A. CHOOSE THE CORRECT WORD

1. stir
   (slice)

2. bake
   boil

3. mix
   grate

4. fry
   carve

5. peel
   pour

6. beat
   cut

B. MATCHING

1.    Chop   the turkey.

2.    Carve   the eggs.

3.    Peel   the onions.

4.   Scramble   the vegetables.

5. Stir-fry   the orange.

FAST FOODS AND SANDWICHES

A. WHAT'S THE WORD?

1. <u>m u f f i n</u>

2. <u>b</u> _ _ _ _ _

3. <u>l</u> _ _ _ _ _ _ _ _

4. _ _ _ _ _ _

5. _ _ _ _ _

6. _ _ _ _ _ _ _ _

7. _ _ _ _ _ _

8. _ _ _

9. _ _ _ _

B. WHICH GROUP?

| coffee | donut | hot dog | hamburger | lemonade | milk | taco | tea |

eat   drink

___taco___   _____ | _____   _____

_____   _____ | _____   _____

C. LISTENING

Listen. Write the number under the correct picture.

___   ___   l   ___   ___

A. CHOOSE THE CORRECT WORD

1. pie
   (cake)

2. nachos
   noodles

3. jello
   ice cream

4. french fries
   potato skins

5. salad
   pudding

6. baked potato
   mashed potatoes

B. WHAT'S ON THE MENU?

Fill in these words to complete the menu.

antipasto

fruit cup

jello

meatloaf

rice

Today's Special Dinner

Appetizer: _____

Salad: _____

Entree: _____

Side Dish: _____

Dessert: _____

COLORS

A. WHAT'S THE COLOR?

1. r e d

2. b _ _ _

3. b _ _ _ _

4. _ _ _ _ _

5. _ _ _ _ _ _

6. _ _ _ _

7. _ _ _ _ _ _

8. _ _ _ _ _

9. _ _ _ _ _

B. CROSSWORD

ACROSS

2.   4.

DOWN

1.   2.   3.

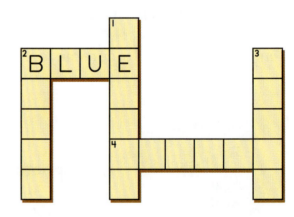

C. JOURNAL

My hair is _____.

My eyes are _____.

My favorite color is _____.

A. WHAT'S THE WORD?

| blouse | jacket | shirt | skirt | sweater |
| dress | pants | shorts | suit | |

1. _____shirt_____

2. _____

3. _____

4. _____

5. _____

6. _____

7. _____

8. _____

9. _____

B. LISTENING

Listen and circle the word you hear.

1. blazer   (blouse)

2. jacket   jumpsuit

3. skirt   shirt

4. necktie   turtleneck

5. suit   shorts

6. jersey   jeans

A. WHAT'S THE WORD?

1. <u>s t o c k i n g s</u>

2. p _ _ _ _ _ _ _

3. <u>s</u> _ _ _ _ _

4. _ _ _ _ _ _

5. _ _ _ _ _ _ _ _

6. _ _ _ _ _

7. _ _ _ _ _ _ _ _

8. _ _ _ _ _ _ _

9. _ _ _ _ _ _ _ _

B. MATCHING

1. hiking   shirt

2. tee   heels

3. boxer   underwear

4. long   boots

5. high   shorts

EXERCISE CLOTHING AND OUTERWEAR

A. WHAT'S THE WORD?

hat	gloves	poncho	rubbers	cap
coat	jacket	mittens	raincoat	

1. ___rubbers___   2. _____   3. _____

4. _____   5. _____   6. _____

7. _____   8. _____   9. _____

B. WHICH GROUP?

gloves	overcoat	poncho	raincoat	rubbers	ski hat

It's raining!   It's cold!

_____poncho_____   _____

_____   _____

_____   _____

JEWELRY AND ACCESSORIES

A. CHOOSE THE CORRECT WORD

1. (earrings)
   cuff links

2. belt
   necklace

3. umbrella
   chain

4. wallet
   watch

5. backpack
   purse

6. ring
   key ring

B. MATCHING

1. wedding	watch
2. wrist	bag
3. change	ring
4. book	necklace
5. cuff	links
6. pearl	purse

DESCRIBING CLOTHING

A. WHAT'S THE WORD?

heavy	high	large	loose	polka-dot	small
striped	light	long	low	short	tight

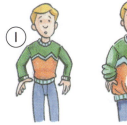  

1. _____tight_____   3. _____   5. _____

2. _____   4. _____   6. _____

7. _____   9. _____   11. _____

8. _____   10. _____   12. _____

B. MATCHING: OPPOSITES

1. long   baggy

2. dark   plain

3. tight   short

4. fancy   narrow

5. wide   light

A. WHICH DEPARTMENT?

1. armchair   Men's Clothing

2. bracelet   Women's Clothing

3. tie   Housewares

4. stove   Furniture

5. iron   Electronics

6. dress   Household Appliances

7. TV   Jewelry

B. MATCHING

1. snack   garage

2. men's   department

3. parking   room

4. water   bar

5. men's clothing   fountain

A. WHAT'S THE WORD?

a. <u>T V</u>

b. _ _ _ _ _ _ _ _ _ _

c. _ _ _

d. _ _ _ _ _ _ _

e. _ _ _ _ _ _ _   _ _ _ _ _ _

f. _ _   _ _ _ _ _ _

g. _ _ _ _   _ _ _ _ _ _ _ _

h. _ _ _ _ _

B. MATCHING

1. tape   contro

2. clock   player

3. video   recorder

4. CD   camera

5. remote   radio

COMPUTERS, TELEPHONES, AND CAMERAS

A. WHAT'S THE WORD?

a. <u>c o m p u t e r</u>

b. _ _ _ _ _ _ _

c. _ _ _ _ _ _ _ _

d. _ _ _ _ _

e. _ _ _ _ _ _ _

f. _ _ _ _ _ _ _ _ _

g. _ _ _ _ _ _ _ _ _ _

h. _ _ _ _ _ _

B. WHICH GROUP?

| film | keyboard | mouse | tripod |
| camera case | modem | printer | zoom lens |

For a camera

film

_____

_____

_____

For a computer

_____

_____

_____

_____

A. WHAT'S THE WORD?

a. <u>b l o c k s</u>

b. _ _ _ _ _ _ _ _

c. _ _ _ _

d. _ _ _ _ _ _ _ _ _

e. _ _ _ _ _ _ _

f. _ _ _ _ _ _ _ _ _ _ _ _ _

g. _ _ _ _ _ _

h. _ _ _ _ _ _ _ _

i. _ _ _ _ _ _ _

j. _ _ _ _ _ _ _ _

k. _ _ _ _ _ _ _ _

l. _ _ _ _ _ _ _ _ _ _

MONEY

A. WHAT IS IT?

| dime | dollar bill | half dollar | nickel | penny | quarter |

1. _____nickel_____

2. _____

3. _____

4. _____

5. _____

6. _____

B. WHAT'S THE VALUE?

| 1¢ | 5¢ | 10¢ | 25¢ | 50¢ | $1.00 |

1. _____10¢_____

4. _____

2. _____

5. _____

3. _____

6. _____

C. MATCHING

1. ten cents $ .50

2. ten dollars $ .01

3. fifty cents $ .10

4. one dollar $10.00

5. one cent $1.00

D. WHAT'S THE AMOUNT?

| $.05 | $.12 | $.15 | $.25 | $.26 | $.30 | $.75 | $15.00 |

1. _____$.05_____   2. _____   3. _____   4. _____

5. _____   6. _____   7. _____   8. _____

E. LISTENING

Listen and circle the amount you hear.

1. $25.00   ($.25)   4. $16.00 $61.00

2. $10.00 $.10   5. $7.10 $71.00

3. $.44 $44.00   6. $14.41 $41.14

A. CHOOSE THE CORRECT WORD

1. bank book
   ~~(check)~~

2. credit card
   checkbook

3. loan application
   money order

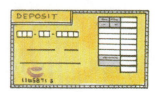

4. deposit slip
   ATM card

5. checkbook
   bank book

6. traveler's check
   withdrawal slip

B. WRITE A CHECK

Write a check to a store.

	Date _December 12, 2001_
Pay to the order of _Acme Discount Store_	$ _30.15_
Thirty and 15/100	Dollars
Memo	_Ana Lopez_
1:2110783	

	Date _____
Pay to the order of _____	$ _____
_____	Dollars
Memo	
1:2110783	

C. AT THE BANK

Your account number is 3758 9402.

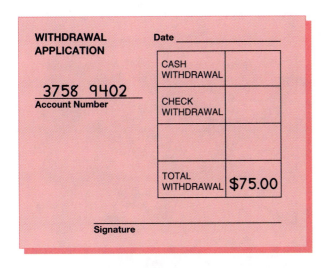

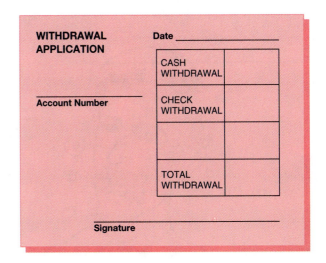

WITHDRAWAL APPLICATION

Date _____

3758 9402
Account Number

CASH WITHDRAWAL	
CHECK WITHDRAWAL	
TOTAL WITHDRAWAL	$75.00

Signature _____

WITHDRAWAL APPLICATION

Date _____

_____
Account Number

CASH WITHDRAWAL	
CHECK WITHDRAWAL	
TOTAL WITHDRAWAL	

Signature _____

1. Withdraw $75.00.

2. Withdraw $200.00.

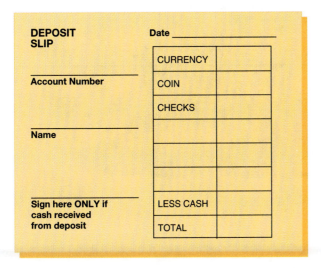

DEPOSIT SLIP

Date _____

_____
Account Number

_____
Name

Sign here ONLY if cash received from deposit _____

CURRENCY	
COIN	
CHECKS	
LESS CASH	
TOTAL	

DEPOSIT SLIP

Date _____

_____
Account Number

_____
Name

Sign here ONLY if cash received from deposit _____

CURRENCY	
COIN	
CHECKS	
LESS CASH	
TOTAL	

3. Deposit $300.00.

4. Deposit $195.00.

A. WHAT IS IT?

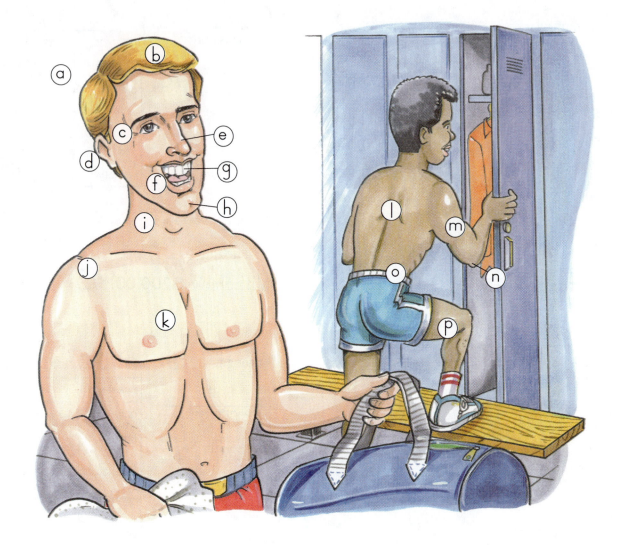

a. <u>h e a d</u>

b. _ _ _ _

c. _ _ _

d. _ _ _

e. _ _ _ _

f. _ _ _ _ _

g. _ _ _ _ _

h. _ _ _ _

i. _ _ _ _

j. _ _ _ _ _ _ _

k. _ _ _ _ _

l. _ _ _ _

m. _ _ _

n. _ _ _ _ _

o. _ _ _ _ _

p. _ _ _

B. WHAT IS IT?

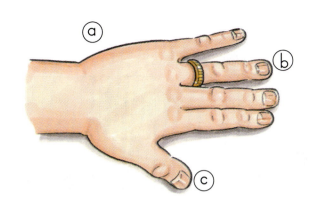

a. <u>h a n d</u>

b. _ _ _ _ _ _

c. _ _ _ _ _ _

d. _ _ _ _

e. _ _ _ _ _

f. _ _ _

C. MATCHING: WHERE ARE THEY?

1. throat — neck
2. finger   foot
3. toe   mouth
4. tooth   arm
5. brain   hand
6. elbow   head

D. HOW MANY DO WE HAVE?

1. feet   ___2___
2. toes   _____
3. stomachs   _____
4. lungs   _____
5. noses   _____

6. fingers   _____
7. hearts   _____
8. thumbs   _____
9. livers   _____
10. eyes   _____

A. CHOOSE THE CORRECT WORD

1. rash
(insect bite)

2. headache
earache

3. stomachache
backache

4. sunburn
fever

5. cough
cavity

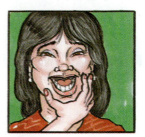

6. wart
toothache

7. cold
rash

8. sore throat
stiff neck

9. the chills
the hiccups

B. LISTENING

Listen and circle the word you hear.

1. earache   (headache)   **4.** rash   virus

2. cold   cough   **5.** fever   cavity

3. stomachache   backache   **6.** chills   hiccups

C. CHOOSE THE CORRECT WORD

1. congested
(dizzy)

2. burn
bruise

3. cut
twist

4. congested
exhausted

5. cough
sprain

D. WORDSEARCH

```
V  F  D  H  R  B  M  P  C  D  I  E  G  H
Q  D  I  V  E  R  M  D  O  O  R  M  S  F
C  Q  Z  I  S  L  F  W  L  P  G  N  N  E
U  L  Z  U  V  H  E  A  D  A  C  H  E  V
A  U  Y  R  A  C  V  L  I  Q  H  U  E  E
T  E  R  W  A  P  E  E  P  A  S  D  Z  W
P  S  U  N  B  U  R  N  O  G  R  C  E  Q
Z  F  N  O  P  W  R  G  S  Q  E  X  H  B
```

✓ COLD   ___ FEVER   ___ SNEEZE

___ DIZZY   ✓ HEADACHE   ___ SUNBURN

E. CROSSWORD

BURN

ACROSS

 3.

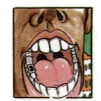 4.

 6.

 7.

 12.

 13.

DOWN

 1.

 2.

 5.

 8.

 9.

 10.

 11.

A. CHOOSE THE CORRECT WORD

1. doctor
   (dentist)

2. pediatrician
   hygienist

3. lab technician
   X-ray technician

4. surgeon
   psychiatrist

5. cardiologist
   optometrist

6. EMT
   nurse

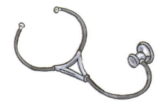

7. drill
   stethoscope

8. thermometer
   needle

9. scale
   X-ray machine

B. MATCHING

1. blood
2. teeth
3. eyes
4. heart
5. children

dentist

optometrist

pediatrician

lab technician

cardiologist

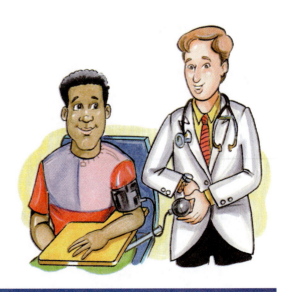

A. CHOOSE THE CORRECT WORD

1. (sling)
   bandaid

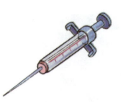

2. prescription
   injection

3. cast
   diet

4. gargle
   exercise

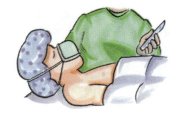

5. surgery
   counseling

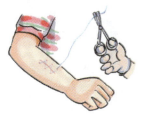

6. crutches
   stitches

7. I.V.
   X-ray

8. bed table
   hospital bed

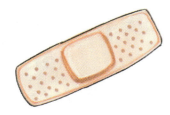

9. medical chart
   bandaid

B. MATCHING

1. physical   tests

2. blood   therapy

3. call   pan

4. bed   gown

5. hospital   button

A. CHOOSE THE CORRECT WORD

1. nasal spray
   (eye drops)

2. aspirin
   cough drops

3. throat lozenges
   antacid tablets

4. cough syrup
   vitamins

5. heating pad
   ice pack

6. ointment
   cold tablets

7. tablet
   capsule

8. pill
   caplet

9. teaspoon
   tablespoon

B. MATCHING

1. cough   spray
2. throat   pad
3. nasal   lozenges
4. heating   tablets
5. antacid   syrup

A. WHAT'S THE WORD?

stamp	mailbox	postcard	air letter	letter
zip code	package	envelope	money order	

1. _____envelope_____   2. _____   3. _____

4. _____   5. _____   6. _____

7. _____   8. _____   9. _____

B. MATCHING

1. letter   address
2. return   order
3. air   carrier
4. money   post
5. parcel   code
6. zip   mail

THE LIBRARY

DICTIONARY
page 76

A. WHAT'S THE WORD?

atlas	magazine	librarian	card catalog
shelves	newspaper	encyclopedia	checkout desk

1. _____librarian_____

2. _____

3. _____

4. _____

5. _____

6. _____

7. _____

8. _____

B. WHICH SECTION OF THE LIBRARY?

dictionary	videotape	tape
newspaper	encyclopedia	magazine

Reference	Periodicals	Media
_____dictionary_____	_____	_____
_____	_____	_____

THE SCHOOL

A. WHERE ARE THEY?

1. The <u>p r i n c i p a l</u> is in

the _ _ _ _ _ _ .

2. The _ _ _ _ _ is in the _ _ _ .

3. The _ _ _ _ _ _ _ _ _ is in

the _ _ _ _ _ _ _ _ _ .

4. The _ _ _ _ _ is in the

_ _ _ _ _ ' _ _ _ _ _ _ _ .

5. The _ _ _ _ _ _ _ _ _

_ _ _ _ _ _ _ _ _ is in the

_ _ _ _ _ _ _ _ _ _ _ _ _ _ .

6. The _ _ _ _ _ _ _ _ is in the

_ _ _ _ _ _ _ _ _ _ _ _ _ .

B. DRAW A DIAGRAM

Draw a picture of your school. Show the different rooms and label them.

A. WHAT'S THE WORD?

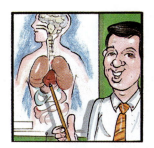

1. <u>h e a l t h</u>

2. h _ _ _ _ _ _

3. F _ _ _ _ _ _

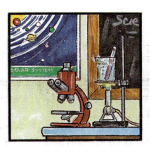

4. <u>b</u> _ _ _

5. <u>s</u> _ _ _ _ _ _

6. <u>m</u> _ _ _

7. _ _ _ _

8. _ _ _ _ _ _

9. _ _ _ _ _ _ _ _

B. WHICH GROUP?

algebra	biology	chemistry	French	geometry	Spanish

Languages	Math	Science
French		

93

A. WHAT'S THE OCCUPATION?

1. b u t c h e r

2. _ _ _ _ _ _ _ _ _

3. _ _ _ _ _ _ _ _

4. _ _ _ _ _ _ _

5. _ _ _ _ _

6. _ _ _ _ _ _

7. _ _ _ _ _ _ _ _ _

8. _ _ _ _ _ _

9. _ _ _ _ _ _ _ _ _ _

10. _ _ _ _ _ _ _ _ _

11. _ _ _ _ _ _ _ _ _

12. _ _ _ _ _ _ _ _ _ _

B. MATCHING: THE SAME JOB

1. journalist   chef
2. janitor   messenger
3. cook   reporter
4. courier   bricklayer
5. mason   custodian

C. MATCHING: WHO USES IT?

1. calculator   carpenter
2. broom   artist
3. hammer   chef
4. saucepan   accountant
5. paintbrush   gardener
6. cash register   custodian
7. rake   barber
8. scissors   cashier

A. WHAT'S THE OCCUPATION?

1. <u>p h a r m a c i s t</u>

2. _ _ _ _ _ _ _

3. _ _ _ _ _ _ _ _ _ _

4. _ _ _ _ _ _ _ _

5. _ _ _ _ _ _ _

6. _ _ _ _ _ _

7. _ _ _ _ _ _ _ _ _

8. _ _ _ _ _ _ _

9. _ _ _ _ _ _ _ _

10. _ _ _ _ _ _ _

11. _ _ _ _ _ _ _ _

12. _ _ _ _ _ _

B. MATCHING: WHO WORKS THERE?

1. garage
2. office
3. school
4. restaurant
5. store
6. drug store

teacher
salesperson
waiter
mechanic
pharmacist
secretary

C. CROSSWORD

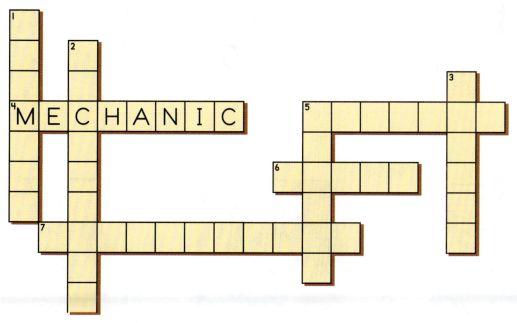

M E C H A N I C

ACROSS

4.

5.

6.

7.

DOWN

1.

2.

3.

5.

A. WHAT DO THEY DO?

1. <u>p a i n t</u>

2. _ _ _ _ _

3. _ _ _ _ _

4. _ _ _ _

5. _ _ _ _ _

6. _ _ _ _

7. _ _ _ _ _ _ _

8. _ _ _ _ _

9. _ _ _ _

10. _ _ _ _ _

11. _ _ _

12. _ _ _ _ _ _ _ _

B. MATCHING

1. Bakers — paint.
2. Actors — build things.
3. Drivers — bake.
4. Painters — assemble components.
5. Assemblers — clean.
6. Carpenters — act.
7. Housekeepers — drive.

C. MATCHING

1. I can guard — food.
2. I can serve — an airplane.
3. I can mow — the piano.
4. I can fly — buildings.
5. I can play — cars.
6. I can sell — lawns.

D. JOURNAL: MY WORK SKILLS

I can _____

_____

_____ .

A. WHAT'S THE WORD?

a. <u>c o a t   r a c k</u>

b. _ _ _ _ _ _ _   _ _ _ _ _

c. _ _ _ _ _ _

d. _ _ _ _ _ _

e. _ _ _ _   _ _ _ _ _ _ _

f. _ _ _ _   _ _ _ _

g. _ _ _ _ _ _   _ _ _ _ _ _

h. _ _ _ _ _   _ _ _ _ _ _

B. MATCHING

1. message   cabinet

2. water   board

3. file   machine

4. employee   cooler

5. copy   lounge

A. CHOOSE THE CORRECT WORD

I. typewriter
(telephone)

2. computer
calculator

3. printer
word processor

4. adding machine
calculator

5. VDT
postal scale

6. paper cutter
paper shredder

B. LISTENING

Listen. Write the correct number.

___ electric pencil sharpener   _1_ telephone

___ typewriter   ___ adding machine

___ fax machine   ___ printer

A. WHAT IS IT?

1. p e n

2. _ _ _ _ _

3. _ _ _ _ _ _ _ _ _ _

4. _ _ _ _ _ _

5. _ _ _ _ _ _

6. _ _ _ _ _ _ _ _ _ _

7. _ _ _ _ _ _ _ _

8. _ _ _ _ _ _ _

9. _ _ _ _ _ _ _ _ _

B. MATCHING

1. wall   cabinet

2. file   opener

3. rubber   calendar

4. swivel   dispenser

5. tape   chair

6. letter   stamp

A. CHOOSE THE CORRECT WORD

1. mailing label
   (envelope)

2. glue
   clamp

3. paper fastener
   paper clip

4. staple
   gluestick

5. message pad
   index card

6. file folder
   stationery

7. rubber cement
   rubber band

8. thumbtack
   plastic clip

9. pushpin
   gluestick

B. MATCHING

1. masking   clip

2. typing   tape

3. paper   card

4. rubber   paper

5. index   band

A. CHOOSE THE CORRECT WORD

1. (time clock)
   work station

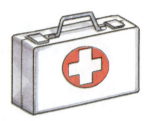

2. suggestion box
   first-aid kit

3. cafeteria
   supply room

4. lever
   forklift

5. conveyor belt
   freight elevator

6. assembly line
   warehouse

7. safety glasses
   masks

8. loading dock
   hand truck

9. suggestion box
   lever

B. MATCHING

1. time   line

2. assembly   station

3. work   clock

4. first-aid   belt

5. conveyor   kit

A. WHAT'S THE WORD?

1. <u>h e l m e t</u>

2. _ _ _ _ _ _

3. _ _ _ _ _ _ _ _ _

4. _ _ _ _ _ _ _

5. _ _ _ _

6. _ _ _ _   _ _ _ _ _

7. _ _ _ _

8. _ _ _ _ _

9. _ _ _ _ _ _ _ _ _ _

B. WHICH GROUP?

beam	pipe	bulldozer
backhoe	plywood	cement mixer

Materials	Machines
beam	

A. WHAT'S THE WORD?

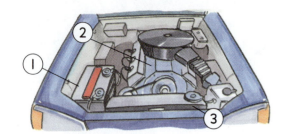

1. <u>b a t t e r y</u>

2. _ _ _ _ _ _

3. _ _ _ _ _ _ _ _ _

4. _ _ _ _

5. _ _ _ _ _ _ _ _ _

6. _ _ _ _ _ _

7. _ _ _ _ _ _ _ _ _ _

8. _ _ _ _ _ _ _

9. _ _ _ _ _ _ _

10. _ _ _ _ _ _

11. _ _ _ _

12. _ _ _ _ _ _ _ _ _

B. MATCHING

1. windshield   plate

2. rear   belt

3. license   defroster

4. spark   wipers

5. fan   plugs

C. CHOOSE THE CORRECT WORD

1. door lock
   (seat belt)

2. steering wheel
   clutch

3. ignition
   accelerator

4. gearshift
   turn signal

5. speedometer
   gas gauge

6. vent
   rearview mirror

7. radio
   horn

8. sedan
   jeep

9. convertible
   minivan

D. MATCHING

1. air   mirror

2. seat   bag

3. rearview   signal

4. turn   brake

5. emergency   belt

A. WHAT'S THE WORD?

1. <u>t o l l b o o t h</u>   2. _ _ _ _ _ _ _   3. _ _ _ _ _ _ _ _ _

4. _ _ _ _ _ _ _ _   5. _ _ _ _ _ _ _   6. _ _ _ _ _ _ _ _ _ _ _ _

7. _ _ _ _ _ _ _ _ _ _   8. _ _ _ _ _ _ _ _ _ _ _ _ _ _

B. LISTENING

Listen. Write the number under the correct sign.

_ _ _   1   _ _ _   _ _ _   _ _ _

PUBLIC TRANSPORTATION

A. WHAT'S THE WORD?

| taxi | subway | bus stop | bus driver | bus |
| train | luggage | conductor | bus station | |

1. ___bus___

2. _____

3. _____

4. _____

5. _____

6. _____

7. _____

8. _____

9. _____

B. MATCHING

1. passenger   compartment

2. cab   driver

3. luggage   station

4. information   car

5. subway   booth

109

A. CHOOSE THE CORRECT WORD

1. (suitcase)
   garment bag

2. gate
   ticket

3. ticket agent
   customs officer

4. passport
   customs

5. security guard
   immigration officer

6. visa
   boarding pass

7. waiting area
   baggage claim area

8. metal detector
   arrival and departure monitor

B. MATCHING

1. immigration   counter

2. security   pass

3. ticket   guard

4. boarding   detector

5. metal   officer

A. CHOOSE THE CORRECT WORD

1. fuselage
   (meal)

2. pilot
   passenger

3. galley
   lavatory

4. life vest
   landing gear

5. helicopter
   prop

6. seat pocket
   seat belt

B. MATScHING

1. emergency   bag

2. seat   exit

3. carry-on   belt

4. flight   compartment

5. overhead   seat

6. window   sign

7. No Smoking   attendant

A. CROSSWORD

³H U R R I C A N E

ACROSS

3.   5.   6.    7.

DOWN

1.    2.   4.

B. JOURNAL

My favorite season is _____

because _____

_____.

OUTDOOR RECREATION

A. CHOOSE THE CORRECT WORD

1. (tent)
   rope

2. camp stove
   lantern

3. compass
   trail map

4. blanket
   sleeping bag

5. harness
   backpack

6. thermos
   hatchet

B. WHAT'S THE WORD?

1. sleeping <u>b</u> <u>a</u> <u>g</u>

2. h _ _ _ _ _ boots

3. t _ _ _ stakes

4. _ _ _ _ _ _ _ basket

5. _ _ _ _ climbing

6. trail _ _ _

C. MATCHING

1. camp   basket

2. trail   bag

3. sleeping   stove

4. hiking   boots

5. picnic   map

THE PARK AND THE PLAYGROUND

A. WHAT'S THE WORD?

| grill | bench | sandbox | trash can | zoo |
| slide | swings | seesaw | rest rooms | |

1. <u>seesaw</u>

2. _____

3. _____

4. _____

5. _____

6. _____

7. _____

8. _____

9. _____

B. MATCHING

1. picnic   can

2. trash   fountain

3. rest   rooms

4. water   rack

5. bike   table

114

A. CHOOSE THE CORRECT WORD

1. bucket
   (shovel)

2. kite
   raft

3. sand dune
   snack bar

4. vendor
   surfer

5. sun hat
   bathing cap

6. lifeguard
   life preserver

7. surfboard
   raft

8. tube
   cooler

9. seashell
   sand castle

B. MATCHING

1. beach
2. suntan
3. bathing
4. life
5. snack

suit
ball
preserver
bar
lotion

A. CROSSWORD

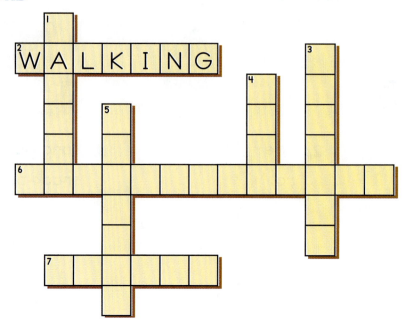

ACROSS

2.

6.

7.

DOWN

1.

3.

4.

5.

B. MATCHING

1. running   pong

2. ping   riding

3. work   shorts

4. horseback   skating

5. roller   out

A. WHAT'S THE SPORT?

baseball	basketball	ice hockey	soccer	football	lacrosse

1. _____football_____   2. _____   3. _____

4. _____   5. _____   6. _____

B. WHICH GROUP?

basketball	ice hockey	soccer	softball	volleyball

field   rink   court

_____   _____   _____

_____   _____   _____

C. JOURNAL

My favorite sport is _____.

My favorite team is _____.

My favorite player is _____.

A. WHAT'S THE WORD?

1. <u>v o l l e y b a l l</u>

2. _ _ _ _ _ _ _ _ _ _   _ _ _

3. _ _ _ _ _ _ _ _ _ _

4. _ _ _ _ _ _ _ _ _

5. _ _ _ _ _ _ _ _

6. _ _ _

7. _ _ _ _ _ _   _ _ _ _

8. _ _ _ _ _ _   _ _ _ _ _

B. LISTENING

Listen. Write the number next to the correct picture.

A. CHOOSE THE CORRECT WORD

1. ski boots
   (ice skates)

2. sled
   bobsled

3. toboggan
   saucer

4. bobsledding
   snowmobiling

5. saucer
   bobsled

6. poles
   bindings

7. cross-country skiing
   downhill skiing

B. MATCHING

1. skate   skiing

2. ice   dish

3. sledding   boots

4. downhill   guards

5. ski   skates

119

A. WHAT'S THE WORD?

1. <u>s w i m m i n g</u>

2. _ _ _ _ _ _ _

3. _ _ _ _ _ _ _

4. _ _ _ _ _ _ _

5. _ _ _ _ _ _ _

6. _ _ _ _ _ _ _ _ _ _

7. _ _ _ _ _ _ _

8. _ _ _ _ _ _ _

9. _ _ _ _ _ _ _ _ _

B. MATCHING

1. mask   rowing

2. rod   swimming

3. oars   fishing

4. paddles   surfing

5. bathing suit   snorkeling

6. surfboard   canoeing

A. CHOOSE THE CORRECT WORD

1. (reach)
   bend

2. kneel
   sit

3. dribble
   kick

4. hit
   pitch

5. shoot
   bounce

6. swing
   lift

7. dive
   dribble

8. serve
   skip

9. push-up
   sit-up

10. leg lift
    handstand

11. jumping jack
    deep knee bend

B. LISTENING

Listen. Write the number under the correct picture.

_____ _____ _____ ____ | _____

A. CHOOSE THE CORRECT WORD

1. (checkers)
   chess

2. marbles
   jacks

3. yarn
   thread

4. photography
   astronomy

5. pottery
   embroidery

6. stamp album
   coin album

7. sculpture
   quilting

8. telescope
   binoculars

9. loom
   sewing machine

B. MATCHING

1. loom   sewing

2. thread   photography

3. clay   weaving

4. camera   astronomy

5. telescope   pottery

A. WHAT'S THE WORD?

1. <u>c o n d u c t o r</u>

2. <u>m</u> _ _ _ _ _ _ _

3. <u>a</u> _ _ _ _ _

4. <u>a</u> _ _ _ _ _ _

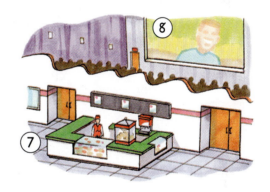

5. _ _ _ _ _ _ _ _ _ _

6. _ _ _ _ _ _ _ _ _

7. _ _ _ _ _ _

8. _ _ _ _ _ _ _

B. MATCHING

1. box   screen

2. ballet   office

3. movie   stand

4. refreshment   orchestra

5. symphony   dancer

A. CHOOSE THE CORRECT WORD

1. bluegrass
   (rock music)

2. musical
   drama

3. western
   comedy

4. jazz
   folk music

5. cartoon
   drama

6. talk show
   game show

B. LISTENING

Listen. Write the number next to the type of music you hear.

___ classical   ___ jazz   ___ reggae   _1_ rap music

___ gospel   ___ country   ___ rock

C. JOURNAL

My favorite TV show is _____.

My favorite movie is _____.

My favorite movie star is _____.

My favorite type of music is _____.

A. CHOOSE THE CORRECT WORD

1. (violin)
   recorder

2. oboe
   drum

3. organ
   piano

4. guitar
   banjo

5. trumpet
   tuba

6. saxophone
   clarinet

B. WHICH GROUP?

| cello | clarinet | flute | trombone | trumpet | violin |

Brass	Strings	Woodwinds
trombone	_____	_____
_____	_____	_____

C. LISTENING

Listen. Write the number next to the instrument you hear.

___ tuba   ___ drum   ___ flute

_1_ harmonica   ___ harp   ___ banjo

A. CHOOSE THE CORRECT WORD

1. twig
(flower)

2. cone
bulb

3. trunk
limb

4. tulip
daisy

5. bark
bush

6. rose
cactus

B. WHAT'S MISSING?

1. t r e <u>e</u>

3. p l _ _ t

5. g r a _ _

2. d o g w _ _ d

4. d a _ _ o d i l

6. f l _ _ e r

C. WHICH GROUP?

| palm | daisy | maple | tulip |
| rose | pine | oak | sunflower |

flowers

_____rose_____

_____

_____

_____

trees

_____

_____

_____

_____

A. CHOOSE THE CORRECT WORD

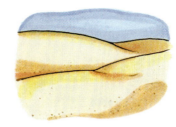

1. (river)
   pond

2. desert
   jungle

3. meadow
   forest

4. dune
   dam

5. seashore
   waterfall

6. lake
   field

B. WHAT'S MISSING?

1. l a k e

2. p _ n d

3. c l i _ _

4. r _ v _ r

5. j _ n _ l e

6. _ c _ _ n

C. MATCHING

1. air   waste

2. toxic   energy

3. natural   pollution

4. nuclear   rain

5. acid   gas

A. WHAT'S THE WORD?

1. <u>f i e l d</u>

2. _ _ _ _ _ _ _

3. _ _ _ _ _ _ _ _

4. _ _ _ _

5. _ _ _ _

6. _ _ _

7. _ _ _ _ _ _

8. _ _ _

9. _ _ _ _ _ _ _

B. MATCHING

1. sheep — lamb
2. cow — piglet
3. chicken — kid
4. goat — chick
5. pig — calf

C. LISTENING

Listen. Write the number next to the farm animal you hear.

| ___ horse | ___ chick | ___ pig | _1_ turkey |
| ___ lamb | ___ rooster | ___ cow | ___ goat |

A. WHAT'S THE WORD?

cat	lion	camel	skunk	rabbit	squirrel
dog	deer	mouse	horse	monkey	elephant

1. _____rabbit_____

2. _____

3. _____

4. _____

5. _____

6. _____

7. _____

8. _____

9. _____

10. _____

11. _____

12. _____

B. LISTENING

Listen. Write the number next to the animal or pet you hear.

___ donkey   ___ bear   ___ dog   ___ hyena

___ mouse   ___ cat   _1_ lion   ___ elephant

BIRDS AND INSECTS

A. WHAT'S THE WORD?

1. <u>r o b i n</u>   2. _ _ _   3. _ _ _ _   4. _ _ _

5. _ _ _ _ _ _   6. _ _ _   7. _ _ _ _ _ _   8. _ _ _ _ _ _

B. WHICH GROUP?

bee	crow	beetle	termite
swan	goose	pigeon	mosquito

Insects

<u>bee</u>   _____   _____   _____

_____   _____   _____   _____

C. LISTENING

Listen. Write the number next to the bird or insect you hear.

___ duck   ___ owl   ___ parrot   ___ crow

___ seagull   ___ bee   _1_ cricket   ___ woodpecker

A. WHAT'S THE WORD?

| crab | snake | shrimp | dolphin | seal |
| frog | whale | turtle | alligator | |

1. _____turtle_____

2. _____

3. _____

4. _____

5. _____

6. _____

7. _____

8. _____

9. _____

B. MATCHING

1. tusk   tortoise

2. shell   octopus

3. flipper   seal

4. claw   walrus

5. tentacle   lobster

A. WHAT'S THE WORD?

line	cube	circle	sphere	pyramid	triangle
cone	angle	square	ellipse	cylinder	rectangle

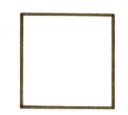

1. _____circle_____

2. _____

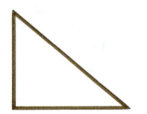

3. _____

4. _____

5. _____

6. _____

7. _____

8. _____

9. _____

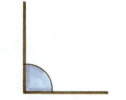

10. _____

11. _____

12. _____

B. WHICH GROUP?

| base   width   length   hypotenuse   radius   diameter |

triangle	circle	rectangle
____base____	_____	_____
_____	_____	_____

C. WHAT'S THE WORD?

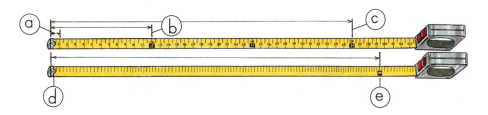

a. i n c h

b. _ _ _ _ _

c. _ _ _ _

d. _ _ _ _ _ _ _ _ _ _

e. _ _ _ _ _

D. MATCHING

1.	cm		mile
2.	m		yard
3.	mi.		centimeter
4.	km		foot
5.	"		meter
6.	'		inch
7.	yd.		kilometer

E. WHAT'S THE ANSWER?

1. 2.54 cm = __1__ "

2. 1' = ___ "

3. 0.914 m = 1 ___

4. 1.6 km = 1 ___

5. 1 yd. = ___ '

6. 0.305 m = ___ '

133

A. WHAT'S THE WORD?

sun	moon	Earth	satellite
star	comet	rocket	astronaut

1. _rocket_   2. _____   3. _____   4. _____

5. _____   6. _____   7. _____   8. _____

B. WHAT'S MISSING?

1. M <u>a</u> r s   3. V _ n _ s   5. N e _ t _ _ e

2. P l u _ o   4. J _ p _ t _ r   6. M e _ c _ r y

C. MATCHING

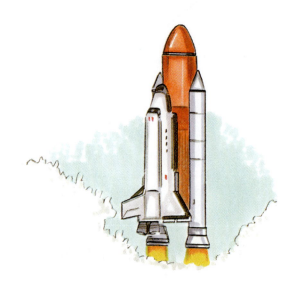

1. space   pad

2. booster   shuttle

3. launch   eclipse

4. lunar   rocket

5. mission   control

WORKBOOK PAGES 1–3

A. CIRCLE THE SAME WORD
1. NAME	4. STATE
2. CITY	5. STREET
3. ADDRESS	

B. MATCHING
1. CA	4. 684-1196
2. 22960	5. NANCY PETERSON
3. MAIN STREET	6. 045-61-8947

F. LISTENING

Listen and circle the words you hear.

1. A. What's your name?
   B. My name? John.
2. A. What's your zip code?
   B. My zip code? 22315.
3. A. What's your social security number?
   B. My social security number? 976-24-3069.
4. A. What's your street?
   B. My street? North Tenth Street.
5. A. What's your city?
   B. My city? Sacramento.
6. A. What's your first name?
   B. My first name? Ana.

Answers
1. name	4. street
2. zip code	5. city
3. social security	6. first

WORKBOOK PAGES 4–5

A. WHO ARE THEY?
1. b	4. e
2. f	5. c
3. d	6. a

B. MATCHING
1. father	4. mother
2. sister	5. son
3. brother	6. daughter

C. WHAT'S MISSING?
1. wife	4. grandson
sister	brother
2. father	5. baby
mother	daughter
3. husband	6. grandmother
son	grandfather

D. WHICH GROUP?
Parents:	Children:
1. father	5. son
2. mother	6. daughter
3. husband	7. brother
4. wife	8. sister

WORKBOOK PAGES 6–7

A. WHO ARE THEY?
1. d	4. e
2. a	5. b
3. c	

B. WHAT'S MISSING?
1. aunt	3. cousin
uncle	son-in-law
2. nephew	4. sister-in-law
niece	brother-in-law

C. WHICH GROUP?
nephew	cousin	aunt
uncle		niece

D. WHO ARE THEY?
1. uncle	5. father
2. aunt	6. aunt
3. nephew	7. uncle
4. niece	8. sister

WORKBOOK PAGE 8

A. THE COMPASS
	north	
west		east
	south	

B. WHERE IS IT?
1. north	4. east
2. south	5. south
3. west	

C. LISTENING

Listen and circle the word you hear.

1. A. Canada is north of the United States.
   B. North?
   A. Yes, that's right.
2. A. Texas is east of New Mexico.
   B. East?
   A. Yes, that's right.
3. A. Nicaragua is south of Honduras.
   B. South?
   A. Yes, that's right.
4. A. Ontario is east of Manitoba.
   B. East?
   A. Yes, that's right.
5. A. Mississippi is in the South.
   B. The South?
   A. Yes, that's right.
6. A. California is in the West.
   B. The West?
   A. Yes, that's right.

Answers
1. north	4. east
2. east	5. south
3. south	6. west

WORKBOOK PAGE 9

A. WHICH CONTINENT?

South America:
Brazil
Peru
Bolivia

Europe:
Poland
Spain
Germany

Africa:
Sudan
Somalia
Morocco

Asia:
Korea
Japan
China

WORKBOOK PAGES 10–11

A. MATCHING

1. take a shower
2. comb my hair
3. go to bed
4. brush my teeth
5. get up
6. take a bath

B. WHAT DO YOU DO EVERY DAY?

1. make
2. brush
3. wash
4. eat
5. shave
6. sleep

C. LISTENING

Listen. Write the correct number.

1. (Sound: bath)
2. (Sound: shower)
3. (Sound: making dinner)
4. (Sound: brushing teeth)
5. (Sound: electric shaver)

Answers

2	3
4	5
1	

WORKBOOK PAGES 12–13

A. LISTENING

Listen. Put a check under the correct picture.

1. A. What's John doing?
   B. He's sweeping the floor.
   A. Sweeping the floor?
   B. Yes.
2. A. What's Carol doing?
   B. She's ironing.
   A. Ironing?
   B. Yes.
3. A. What's Maria doing?
   B. She's listening to the radio.
   A. Listening to the radio?
   B. Yes.
4. A. What's your brother doing?
   B. He's washing the dishes.
   A. Washing the dishes?
   B. Yes.
5. A. What's Peter doing?
   B. He's doing the laundry.
   A. Doing the laundry?
   B. Yes.

6. A. What's your cousin doing?
   B. She's feeding the baby.
   A. Feeding the baby?
   B. Yes.

Answers

1.	✓	___		2.	___	✓
3.	___	✓		4.	✓	___
5.	✓	___		6.	___	✓

B. MATCHING

1. the dishes
2. basketball
3. TV
4. the cat

C. WHAT DO YOU DO EVERY DAY?

1. study
2. watch TV
3. dust
4. exercise
5. play
6. vacuum

D. LISTENING

Listen. Write the correct number.

1. (Sound: exercising/counting)
2. (Sound: basketball bouncing)
3. (Sound: broom sweeping floor)
4. (Sound: washing machine)
5. (Sound: washing dishes)
6. (Sound: vacuum cleaner)

Answers

3	5
6	4
1	2

WORKBOOK PAGES 14–15

A. WHAT'S THE WORD?

a. clock
b. teacher
c. map
d. book
e. pencil
f. desk
g. notebook
h. student
i. ruler
j. board

B. LISTENING

Listen and circle the word you hear.

1. A. Where's the pencil?
   B. The pencil? It's on the desk.
2. A. Where's the paper?
   B. The paper? It's on the bookshelf.
3. A. Where's the chalk?
   B. The chalk? It's on the teacher's desk.
4. A. Where's the ruler?
   B. The ruler? It's on my desk.
5. A. Where's your notebook?
   B. My notebook? It's in my desk.
6. A. Where's the computer?
   B. The computer? It's next to the TV.

Answers

1. pencil
2. paper
3. chalk
4. ruler
5. notebook
6. computer

C. WHAT'S IN THE CLASSROOM?

1. clock
2. globe
3. book
4. map
5. computer

WORKBOOK PAGES 16–17

A. LISTENING

Listen. Put a check under the correct picture.

1. A. Please write your name.
   B. Write my name? Sure.
2. A. Please close your book.
   B. Close my book? Sure.
3. A. Please help each other.
   B. Help each other? Okay.
4. A. Please hand in your homework.
   B. Hand in my homework? Okay.
5. A. Please answer the questions.
   B. Answer the questions? Okay.
6. A. Please turn off the lights.
   B. Turn off the lights? Sure.

Answers
1. ✓ ___   2. ___ ✓
3. ✓ ___   4. ✓ ___
5. ✓ ___   6. ___ ✓

B. MATCHING

1. up.
2. your name.
3. your book.
4. down.

C. WHAT'S THE ACTION?

1. Write
2. Go
3. Close
4. Watch
5. Raise
6. Do
7. Turn off
8. Work

WORKBOOK PAGE 18

A. MATCHING

1. Mexican   Spanish
2. Chinese   Chinese
3. Haitian   Haitian Kreyol
4. Cambodian   Cambodian
5. Ethiopian   Amharic

B. LISTENING

Listen and circle the country you hear.

1. A. Where are you from?
   B. Thailand.
   A. Thailand?
   B. Yes.
2. A. Where are you from?
   B. Russia.
   A. Russia?
   B. Yes.
3. A. Where are you from?
   B. Portugal.
   A. Portugal?
   B. Yes.
4. A. Where are you from?
   B. I'm from Estonia.
   A. Estonia?
   B. Yes.
5. A. Where are you from?
   B. I'm from Canada.
   A. Canada?
   B. Yes.
6. A. Where are you from?
   B. Ecuador.
   A. Ecuador?
   B. Yes.

Answers
1. Thailand   4. Estonia
2. Russia   5. Canada
3. Portugal   6. Ecuador

WORKBOOK PAGE 19

A. CHOOSE THE CORRECT ANSWER

1. b   2. a
3. a   4. b

B. WHAT TYPE OF HOUSING?

1. cabin   2. trailer   3. house
4. farmhouse   5. apartment   6. shelter

WORKBOOK PAGES 20–21

A. CIRCLE THE CORRECT WORD

1. armchair   2. bookcase   3. rug
4. plant   5. floor   6. painting

B. WHERE IS IT?

1. lamp   4. painting
2. picture   5. pillow
3. drapes

C. WHAT'S THE WORD?

1. sofa   2. rug   3. lamp
4. window   5. bookcase   6. plant
7. television   8. fireplace   9. pillow

WORKBOOK PAGE 22

A. WHAT'S IN THE DINING ROOM?

1. candle   2. table   3. chair
4. pitcher   5. teapot

B. MATCHING

1. cabinet   4. bowl
2. shaker   5. pot
3. dish

C. LISTENING

Listen and circle the words you hear.

1. A. Please pass the butter dish.
   B. The butter dish? Here you are.
2. A. Please pass the pitcher.
   B. The pitcher? Here you are.
3. A. May I have the salt shaker, please?
   B. The salt shaker? Here you are.

4. A. I really like your tablecloth.
  B. My tablecloth? Thank you very much.
5. A. I really like your teapot.
  B. My teapot? Thank you very much.
6. A. I really like your sugar bowl.
  B. My sugar bowl? Thank you very much.

Answers

1. butter dish	4. tablecloth
2. pitcher	5. teapot
3. salt shaker	6. sugar bowl

WORKBOOK PAGE 23

A. CHOOSE THE CORRECT ANSWER

1. a	2. b
3. b	4. a

B. WHAT IS IT?

1. glass	2. cup	3. napkin
4. teaspoon	5. knife	6. fork

WORKBOOK PAGES 24–25

A. WHAT'S THE WORD?

1. pillow	2. bed	3. mirror
4. dresser	5. blanket	6. blinds

B. MATCHING

1. table	4. bed
2. clock	5. radio
3. box	6. spring

C. WHERE IS IT?

1. nightstand	4. chest
2. bed	5. mirror
3. dresser	6. blinds

D. LISTENING

Listen and circle the words you hear.

1. A. Ooh! There's a big bug on the blanket.
  B. On the blanket? I'll get it.
2. A. Ooh! There's a big bug on the dresser.
  B. On the dresser? I'll get it.
3. A. Excuse me. I'm looking for a bedspread.
  B. We have some very nice bedspreads on sale this week.
4. A. Excuse me. I'm looking for a mirror.
  B. We have some very nice mirrors on sale this week.
5. A. Oh, no! I just lost my contact lens! I think it's on the pillow.
  B. On the pillow? I'll help you look.
6. A. I'm looking for a clock radio.
  B. Clock radios are over there.
  A. Thank you.

Answers

1. blanket	4. mirror
2. dresser	5. pillow
3. bedspread	6. clock radio

WORKBOOK PAGE 26

A. WHAT'S IN THE KITCHEN?

1. dishwasher	2. oven	3. toaster
4. cabinet	5. sink	6. stove
7. microwave	8. sponge	9. refrigerator

B. WHICH GROUP?

For cooking:	For cleaning:
microwave	dishwasher
range	sink

WORKBOOK PAGE 27

A. WHAT IS IT?

1. grater	2. pot	3. wok
4. blender	5. ladle	6. saucepan

B. MATCHING

1. plate	4. opener
2. kettle	5. pan
3. maker	

C. LISTENING

Listen. Write the correct number.

1. (Sound: blender)
2. (Sound: sizzling bacon in frying pan)
3. (Sound: mixer)
4. (Sound: popcorn maker)
5. (Sound: manual can opener)
6. (Sound: tea kettle whistling)

Answers

3	2
6	5
1	4

WORKBOOK PAGE 28

A. WHAT IS IT?

1. stroller	2. crib	3. doll
4. car seat	5. swing	6. high chair

B. MATCHING

1. in the toy chest.	4. in the playpen.
2. in the crib.	5. on the changing table.
3. on the chest.	

WORKBOOK PAGE 29

A. WHAT IS IT?

1. ointment	2. bottle	3. nipple
4. bib	5. pacifier	6. baby food

B. MATCHING

1. powder	4. swabs
2. pins	5. diapers
3. ring	

C. LISTENING

Listen. Write the number under the correct picture.

1. A. Where's the ointment?
  B. The ointment? It's on the changing table.

2. A. Where are the baby wipes?
   B. The baby wipes? They're on the changing table.
3. A. Where are the diaper pins?
   B. The diaper pins? They're on the changing table.
4. A. Where's the pacifier?
   B. The pacifier? It's in the crib.
5. A. Where's the bib?
   B. The bib? It's in the kitchen.
6. A. Where's the baby shampoo?
   B. The baby shampoo? It's on the changing table.

Answers

2   6   1   4   3   5

WORKBOOK PAGE 30

A. WHAT'S IN THE BATHROOM?
1. plunger   2. toothbrush   3. mirror
4. bathtub   5. sink   6. soap
7. shower   8. toilet   9. bath mat

B. LISTENING
Listen and circle the word you hear.
1. A. Did you clean the mirror?
   B. The mirror? No, not yet.
2. A. Did you clean the sink?
   B. The sink? No, not yet.
3. A. Did you clean the shower?
   B. The shower? No, not yet.
4. A. Did you clean the toilet?
   B. The toilet? No, not yet.
5. A. Did you clean the sponge?
   B. The sponge? No, not yet.
6. A. Did you clean the tub?
   B. The tub? No, not yet.

Answers
1. mirror   4. toilet
2. sink   5. sponge
3. shower   6. tub

WORKBOOK PAGE 31

A. WHAT IS IT?
1. comb   2. razor   3. toothbrush
4. shampoo   5. scissors   6. hair brush

B. WHICH GROUP?

For teeth:
dental floss
mouthwash
toothbrush
toothpaste

For hair:
brush
comb
conditioner
shampoo

C. LISTENING
Listen. Write the correct number.
1. A. Did you remember to pack your hair brush?
   B. My hair brush? Oops! I forgot.

2. A. Did you remember to pack your shampoo?
   B. My shampoo? Oops! I forgot.
3. A. Did you remember to pack your comb?
   B. My comb? No, I forgot.
4. A. Did you remember to pack your powder?
   B. My powder? No, I forgot.
5. A. Did you remember to pack your toothpaste?
   B. My toothpaste? Yes.
6. A. Did you remember to pack your scissors?
   B. My scissors? Yes.

Answers
3   6   2
4   1   5

WORKBOOK PAGE 32

A. WHAT IS IT?
1. broom   2. mop   3. dustpan
4. iron   5. hanger   6. bucket

B. MATCHING
1. next to the dryer.   4. on the clothesline.
2. next to the dustpan.   5. on the dryer.
3. next to the utility sink.

C. LISTENING
Listen and circle the words you hear.
1. A. Excuse me. I'm looking for bleach.
   B. Bleach? We have bleach at the back of the store.
2. A. Excuse me. I'm looking for an iron.
   B. An iron? We have irons at the back of the store.
3. A. Excuse me. I'm looking for a dry mop.
   B. A dry mop? We have dry mops at the back of the store.
4. A. Excuse me. I'm looking for cleanser.
   B. Cleanser? It's at the back of the store.
5. A. Excuse me. I'm looking for a bucket.
   B. Buckets are at the back of the store.
6. A. Excuse me. I'm looking for a sponge.
   B. Sponges are at the back of the store.

Answers
1. bleach   4. cleanser
2. iron   5. bucket
3. dry mop   6. sponge

WORKBOOK PAGE 33

A. WHAT IS IT?
1. mailbox   2. garage   3. lamppost
4. lawnmower   5. window   6. chimney

B. MATCHING
1. door   4. lawnmower
2. mailbox   5. garage
3. TV antenna

WORKBOOK PAGE 34

A. CHOOSE THE CORRECT WORD
1. fire alarm   2. buzzer   3. elevator
4. balcony   5. laundry room   6. parking lot

B. MATCHING
1. room
2. pool
3. lot
4. detector
5. chute
6. conditioner

WORKBOOK PAGE 35

A. WHO IS IT?
1. locksmith   2. painter   3. carpenter
4. plumber   5. gardener   6. electrician

B. MATCHING: WHO REPAIRS IT?
1. TV repair person
2. plumber
3. carpenter
4. electrician
5. locksmith

WORKBOOK PAGE 36

A. WHAT IS IT?
1. saw   2. hammer   3. pliers
4. wrench   5. drill   6. screwdriver

B. MATCHING
1. bit
2. screw
3. nail
4. bolt
5. brush

C. LISTENING
Listen. Write the correct number.
1. (Sound: electric drill)
2. (Sound: hammer)
3. (Sound: power saw)
4. (Sound: sandpaper)
5. (Sound: saw)
6. (Sound: scraper)

Answers

2	4
5	1
6	3

WORKBOOK PAGE 37

A. WHAT IS IT?
1. plunger   2. shovel   3. flashlight
4. hose   5. rake   6. mousetrap

B. MATCHING
1. hose
2. clippers
3. seeds
4. swatter
5. measure
6. cord

WORKBOOK PAGES 38–39

A. MATCHING
1. three   3
2. eight   8
3. seven   7
4. six   6
5. five   5

B. WHAT'S THE NUMBER?
1. 9
2. 3
3. 16
4. 12
5. 70

C. WHAT'S THE WORD?
four
six
thirteen
forty
one hundred

D. LISTENING
Listen and circle the number you hear.
1. A. How old is your daughter?
   B. She's thirteen years old.
   A. Thirteen?
   B. Yes.
2. A. How old is your son?
   B. He's forty years old.
   A. Forty?
   B. Yes.
3. A. How old is he?
   B. He's seventy years old.
   A. Seventy?
   B. Yes.
4. A. How old is she?
   B. She's sixteen years old.
   A. Sixteen?
   B. Yes.
5. A. How old are you?
   B. I'm twenty-four years old.
   A. Twenty-four?
   B. Yes.
6. A. How old are you?
   B. I'm thirty-five years old.
   A. Thirty-five?
   B. Yes.

Answers

1. 13	3. 70	5. 24
2. 40	4. 16	6. 35

E. MATCHING
1. 3rd   6. 11th
2. 9th   7. 8th
3. 1st   8. 4th
4. 12th   9. 80th
5. 60th   10. 14th

F. WHAT'S THE NUMBER?
1. 2nd   4. 1st
2. 10th   5. 50th
3. 13th   6. 3rd

G. WHAT'S THE WORD?

fourteenth
sixth
sixtieth
eleventh
twentieth
twenty-first

H. MATCHING

1. fourth
2. fifth
3. second
4. first
5. third
6. tenth

I. LISTENING

Listen and circle the number you hear.

1. A. What floor do you live on?
   B. I live on the fourteenth floor.
   A. The fourteenth?
   B. Yes.
2. A. What floor do you live on?
   B. I live on the seventh floor.
   A. The seventh?
   B. Yes.
3. A. What floor do you live on?
   B. I live on the thirtieth floor.
   A. The thirtieth?
   B. Yes.
4. A. What floor do you live on?
   B. The eighteenth floor.
   A. The eighteenth?
   B. Yes.
5. A. What floor do you live on?
   B. The twenty-second floor.
   A. The twenty-second?
   B. Yes.

Answers

1. 14th
2. 7th
3. 30th
4. 18th
5. 22nd

WORKBOOK PAGES 40–41

A. MATCHING

1. multiplication
2. division
3. subtraction
4. addition

B. MATCHING

1. –
2. x
3. =
4. +
5. ÷

C. LISTENING

Listen and circle the answer.

1. A. How much is three times two?
   B. Three times two equals six.
2. A. How much is four plus five?
   B. Four plus five equals nine.
3. A. How much is nine divided by three?
   B. Nine divided by three equals three.
4. A. How much is eight minus two?
   B. Eight minus two equals six.
5. A. How much is two times five?
   B. Two times five equals ten.

Answers

1. x
2. +
3. ÷
4. –
5. x

D. WRITE THE MATH PROBLEMS

1. $\begin{array}{r} 1 \\ +3 \\ \hline 4 \end{array}$
2. $8 \div 4 = 2$
3. $2 \times 5 = 10$
4. $\begin{array}{r} 12 \\ -7 \\ \hline 5 \end{array}$

E. WHAT'S THE FRACTION?

1/4   1/2   1/3   2/3   3/4

F. MATCHING

1. 1/2
2. 1/4
3. 2/3
4. 3/4
5. 1/3

G. LISTENING

Listen and circle the answer.

1. A. Is this on sale?
   B. Yes. It's one third off the regular price.
   A. One third off the regular price?
   B. That's right.
2. A. Is this on sale?
   B. Yes. It's one half off the regular price.
   A. One half off the regular price?
   B. That's right.
3. A. Is this on sale?
   B. Yes. It's one quarter off the regular price.
   A. One quarter off the regular price?
   B. That's right.
4. A. The gas tank is three quarters full.
   B. Three quarters?
   A. Yes.
5. A. The gas tank is half full.
   B. Half full?
   A. Yes.

Answers

1. 1/3
2. 1/2
3. 1/4
4. 3/4
5. 1/2

H. WHAT'S THE PERCENT?

75%   25%   50%   100%

I. MATCHING

1. 50%
2. 25%
3. 100%
4. 30%
5. 75%

J. LISTENING

Listen and write the percent you hear.

1. A. There's a fifty percent chance of rain.
   B. Fifty percent?
   A. Yes.
2. A. There's a one hundred percent chance of rain.
   B. One hundred percent?
   A. Yes.
3. A. How did you do on the test?
   B. I got ninety percent of the answers right.
   A. Ninety percent?
   B. Yes.
4. A. How did you do on the test?
   B. I got seventy-five percent of the answers right.
   A. Seventy-five percent?
   B. Yes.
5. A. Is this on sale?
   B. Yes. It's twenty-five percent off the regular price.
   A. Twenty-five percent?
   B. Yes. That's right.
6. A. Is this on sale?
   B. Yes. It's ten percent off the regular price.
   A. Ten percent?
   B. Yes. That's right.

Answers
1. 50%   4. 75%
2. 100%   5. 25%
3. 90%   6. 10%

WORKBOOK PAGES 42–43

A. WHAT TIME IS IT?

| 8:00 | 2:15 | 6:45 | 4:30 |
| 5:05 | 10:20 | 12:55 | 6:40 |

B. CHOOSE THE CORRECT ANSWER
1. a   2. b
3. a   4. b

C. MATCHING
1. 3:45   three forty-five
2. 4:20   twenty after four
3. 4:30   four thirty
4. 4:15   four fifteen
5. 4:50   ten to five

D. CHOOSE THE CORRECT TIME
1. 7:00 A.M.   3. noon
2. midnight   4. 10:00 P.M.

E. LISTENING

Listen and circle the time you hear.

1. A. What time does the train leave?
   B. At eight thirty.
   A. Eight thirty? Thanks.
2. A. What time does the train leave?
   B. At ten o'clock.
   A. Ten o'clock? Thanks.

3. A. When does the bus leave?
   B. At three fifteen.
   A. Three fifteen? Thanks.
4. A. When does the bus leave?
   B. At six forty-five.
   A. Six forty-five? Thanks.
5. A. When will we arrive?
   B. At half past one.
   A. Half past one? Thanks.
6. A. When will we arrive?
   B. At one oh five.
   A. One oh five? Thanks.

Answers
1. 8:30   4. 6:45
2. 10:00   5. 1:30
3. 3:15   6. 1:05

WORKBOOK PAGES 44–45

A. WHAT'S MISSING?
1. January   7. July
2. February   8. August
3. March   9. September
4. April   10. October
5. May   11. November
6. June   12. December

B. WRITE THE MONTH
1. February   4. September
2. May   5. December
3. July

C. WHAT'S MISSING?
1. Sunday   5. Thursday
2. Monday   6. Friday
3. Tuesday   7. Saturday
4. Wednesday

D. WRITE THE DAY
1. Sunday   5. Thursday
2. Monday   6. Friday
3. Tuesday   7. Saturday
4. Wednesday

E. MATCHING
1. July 10, 1998   4. February 1, 1999
2. May 8, 1999   5. March 6, 1997
3. January 2, 1999

G. LISTENING

Listen and circle the correct answer.

1. A. What day is it?
   B. It's Monday.
   A. Monday? Thanks.
2. A. What day is it?
   B. Tuesday.
   A. Tuesday? Thanks.
3. A. What month is it?
   B. June.
   A. June? Thanks.

4. A. What month is it?
   B. It's December.
   A. December? Thanks.
5. A. What's today's date?
   B. Today is April fourth.
   A. April fourth? Thanks.
6. A. When is your birthday?
   B. My birthday is on March seventh.
   A. March seventh?
   B. Yes.

Answers
1. Monday
2. Tuesday
3. June
4. December
5. April 4
6. March 7

WORKBOOK PAGES 46–47

A. WHAT'S THE PLACE?
1. clinic
2. bakery
3. bank
4. grocery store
5. hair salon
6. drug store
7. bus station
8. gas station
9. coffee shop
10. book store
11. hardware store
12. hospital

B. MATCHING
1. florist
2. service station
3. pharmacy
4. car dealer
5. day-care center

C. MATCHING
1. hardware store
2. bank
3. barber shop
4. gas station
5. cafeteria

D. LISTENING
Listen and circle the place you hear.
1. A. Where are you going?
   B. To the coffee shop.
   A. The coffee shop?
   B. Yes.
2. A. Where are you going?
   B. To the book store.
   A. The book store?
   B. Yes.
3. A. Where are you going?
   B. To the hardware store.
   A. The hardware store?
   B. Yes.
4. A. Where are you going?
   B. To the appliance store.
   A. The appliance store?
   B. Yes.
5. A. Where are you going?
   B. To the copy center.
   A. The copy center?
   B. Yes.
6. A. Where are you going?
   B. To the gas station.
   A. The gas station?
   B. Yes.

Answers
1. coffee shop
2. book store
3. hardware store
4. appliance store
5. copy center
6. gas station

WORKBOOK PAGES 48–49

A. WHAT'S THE PLACE?
1. museum
2. park
3. library
4. school
5. restaurant
6. post office
7. garage
8. laundromat
9. hotel
10. mall
11. supermarket
12. parking lot

B. MATCHING
1. library
2. post office
3. school
4. restaurant
5. parking lot

C. WORDSEARCH (see p. 154)

WORKBOOK PAGES 50–51

A. WHAT'S THE WORD?
1. meter maid
2. meter
3. bus
4. bus stop
5. taxi
6. taxi driver
7. pedestrian
8. police officer
9. traffic light
10. street sign
11. sewer
12. sidewalk

B. MATCHING
1. station
2. meter
3. booth
4. light
5. container

C. WHICH GROUP?

People:	Places:
bus driver	bus stop
pedestrian	intersection
police officer	police station
taxi driver	taxi stand

D. YES OR NO?
1. No
2. Yes
3. No
4. Yes
5. No

WORKBOOK PAGES 52–53

A. WHAT'S THE WORD?
1. new
2. old
3. tall
4. short
5. empty
6. full
7. open
8. closed
9. clean
10. dirty
11. large
12. small

B. MATCHING: OPPOSITES
1. slow
2. little
3. light
4. low
5. tight
6. narrow
7. young
8. bad
9. light
10. cold

C. WHAT'S THE WORD?

1. short
2. single
3. narrow
4. cold
5. plain
6. heavy
7. dull

WORKBOOK PAGES 54–55

A. LISTENING

Listen. Put a check under the correct picture.

1. A. You look sad.
   B. I am. I'm VERY sad.
2. A. You look cold.
   B. I am. I'm VERY cold.
3. A. You look thirsty.
   B. I am. I'm VERY thirsty.
4. A. You look worried.
   B. I am. I'm VERY worried.
5. A. You look sick.
   B. I am. I'm VERY sick.
6. A. Are you disappointed?
   B. Yes. I'm VERY disappointed.
7. A. Are you happy?
   B. Yes. I'm VERY happy.
8. A. Are you angry?
   B. Yes. I'm VERY angry.
9. A. Are you nervous?
   B. Yes. I'm VERY nervous.
10. A. Are you confused?
    B. Yes. I'm VERY confused.

Answers

1.	___	✓	2.	✓	___
3.	✓	___	4.	___	✓
5.	___	✓	6.	___	✓
7.	✓	___	8.	✓	___
9.	___	✓	10.	___	✓

B. CHOOSE THE CORRECT WORD

1. proud
2. happy
3. tired
4. upset
5. ashamed
6. jealous

C. WHICH GROUP?

"happy" words:	"sad" words:
ecstatic	miserable
pleased	unhappy
proud	upset

WORKBOOK PAGE 56

A. WHAT'S THE WORD?

1. lemon
2. pear
3. apple
4. plum
5. lime
6. banana
7. orange
8. peach
9. grapes

B. LISTENING

Listen and circle the fruit you hear.

1. A. Do we have any cherries?
   B. Cherries? Yes.
2. A. Do we have any lemons?
   B. Lemons? Yes.
3. A. Do we have any prunes?
   B. Prunes? Yes.
4. A. Do you like the papaya?
   B. Yes. This papaya is delicious.
5. A. Do you like the grapes?
   B. Yes. These grapes are delicious.
6. A. Do you like the tangerine?
   B. Yes. This tangerine is delicious.

Answers

1. cherries
2. lemons
3. prunes
4. papaya
5. grapes
6. tangerine

WORKBOOK PAGE 57

A. WHAT'S THE WORD?

1. onion
2. tomato
3. carrot
4. lettuce
5. radish
6. mushroom
7. corn
8. potato
9. cucumber

B. MATCHING

1. squash
2. pepper
3. potato
4. bean
5. sprout

WORKBOOK PAGES 58–59

A. WHAT'S THE WORD?

1. milk
2. cheese
3. rice
4. butter
5. soda
6. yogurt
7. cereal
8. cookies
9. spaghetti
10. eggs
11. soup
12. orange juice

B. WHAT'S THE WORD?

1. rolls
2. chicken
3. steak
4. bread
5. cake
6. ice cream

C. WHICH GROUP?

Dairy Products:	Canned Goods:	Packaged Goods:
margarine	soup	crackers
sour cream	tuna fish	macaroni

Meat:	Poultry:	Seafood:
ham	duck	shrimp
pork	turkey	trout

WORKBOOK PAGES 60–61

A. CHOOSE THE CORRECT WORD

1. mustard
2. ham
3. salt
4. olive oil
5. napkins
6. mozzarella
7. soap
8. popcorn
9. peanuts
10. coffee
11. paper bag
12. scale

B. MATCHING

1. cheese
2. sauce
3. dressing
4. mix
5. towels
6. beef
7. chips
8. oil
9. bags
10. food

C. WHICH GROUP?

Deli:	Snack Foods:	Condiments:
turkey	peanuts	ketchup
roast beef	potato chips	pickles

Baking Products:	Paper Products:	Household Items:
flour	napkins	soap
sugar	tissues	trash bags

WORKBOOK PAGES 62–63

A. WHAT'S THE WORD?

1. dozen
2. can
3. bag
4. jar
5. head
6. bunch
7. box
8. pound
9. loaf
10. bar
11. quart
12. pint
13. gallon
14. bottle

B. MATCHING

1. jelly
2. cereal
3. soda
4. bananas
5. tuna fish
6. eggs
7. paper towels

C. WORDSEARCH (see p. 154)

WORKBOOK PAGE 64

A. MATCHING

1. tablespoon
2. pint
3. gallon
4. pound
5. ounce
6. teaspoon
7. fluid ounce

B. WHAT'S THE NUMBER?

1. 8
2. 64
3. 1
4. 16
5. 32

C. LISTENING

Listen and circle the amount you hear.

1. A. How much milk should I put in?
   B. The recipe says to add one ounce.
   A. One ounce?
   B. Yes.
2. A. How much water should I put in?
   B. The recipe says to add one teaspoon.
   A. One teaspoon?
   B. Yes.
3. A. How much flour should I put in?
   B. The recipe says to add one pound of flour.
   A. One pound?
   B. Yes.
4. A. How much roast beef would you like?
   B. Eight ounces, please.
   A. Eight ounces?
   B. Yes, please.
5. A. How much cheese would you like?
   B. Three quarters of a pound, please.
   A. Three quarters of a pound?

   B. Yes.
6. A. How much milk should I put in?
   B. A cup.
   A. A cup?
   B. Yes. A cup.

Answers

1. ounce
2. tsp.
3. lb.
4. 8 ozs.
5. 3/4 lb.
6. cup

WORKBOOK PAGE 65

A. CHOOSE THE CORRECT WORD

1. slice
2. bake
3. grate
4. fry
5. pour
6. beat

B. MATCHING

1. the onions.
2. the turkey.
3. the orange.
4. the eggs.
5. the vegetables.

WORKBOOK PAGE 66

A. WHAT'S THE WORD?

1. muffin
2. bagel
3. lemonade
4. coffee
5. donut
6. hamburger
7. hot dog
8. tea
9. milk

B. WHICH GROUP?

eat:		drink:	
taco	hot dog	coffee	milk
donut	hamburger	lemonade	tea

C. LISTENING

Listen. Write the number under the correct picture.

1. A. May I help you?
   B. Yes. I'd like a cheeseburger, please.
   A. A cheeseburger?
   B. Yes.
2. A. May I help you?
   B. Yes. I'd like a slice of pizza, please.
   A. A slice of pizza?
   B. Yes.
3. A. May I help you?
   B. Yes. I'd like a bacon, lettuce, and tomato sandwich, please.
   A. A bacon, lettuce, and tomato sandwich?
   B. Yes.
4. A. May I help you?
   B. Yes. I'd like an order of fried chicken, please.
   A. An order of fried chicken?
   B. Yes.
5. A. May I help you?
   B. Yes. I'd like a bowl of chili, please.
   A. A bowl of chili?
   B. Yes.
6. A. May I help you?
   B. Yes. I'd like an iced tea, please.
   A. An iced tea?
   B. Yes.

3 5 1 6 4 2

WORKBOOK PAGE 67

A. CHOOSE THE CORRECT WORD

1. cake
2. nachos
3. ice cream
4. potato skins
5. salad
6. baked potato

B. WHAT'S ON THE MENU?

antipasto
fruit cup
meatloaf
rice
jello

WORKBOOK PAGE 68

A. WHAT'S THE COLOR?

1. red
2. blue
3. brown
4. green
5. yellow
6. pink
7. orange
8. black
9. white

B. CROSSWORD (see p. 154)

WORKBOOK PAGE 69

A. WHAT'S THE WORD?

1. shirt
2. suit
3. blouse
4. jacket
5. pants
6. skirt
7. sweater
8. dress
9. shorts

B. LISTENING

Listen and circle the word you hear.

1. A. Do you like my new blouse?
   B. Yes. It's a very nice blouse.
2. A. Do you like my new jacket?
   B. Yes. It's a very nice jacket.
3. A. Do you like my new shirt?
   B. Yes. It's a very nice shirt.
4. A. Do you like my new necktie?
   B. Yes. It's a very nice necktie.
5. A. Do you like my new suit?
   B. Yes. It's a very nice suit.
6. A. Do you like my new jeans?
   B. Yes. They're very nice jeans.

Answers

1. blouse
2. jacket
3. shirt
4. necktie
5. suit
6. jeans

WORKBOOK PAGE 70

A. WHAT'S THE WORD?

1. stockings
2. pajamas
3. shoes
4. socks
5. bathrobe
6. boots
7. sneakers
8. sandals
9. nightgown

B. MATCHING

1. boots
2. shirt
3. shorts
4. underwear
5. heels

WORKBOOK PAGE 71

A. WHAT'S THE WORD?

1. rubbers
2. jacket
3. hat
4. poncho
5. raincoat
6. gloves
7. coat
8. mittens
9. cap

B. WHICH GROUP?

It's raining!	It's cold!
poncho	gloves
raincoat	overcoat
rubbers	ski hat

WORKBOOK PAGE 72

A. CHOOSE THE CORRECT WORD

1. earrings
2. necklace
3. umbrella
4. watch
5. backpack
6. ring

B. MATCHING

1. ring
2. watch
3. purse
4. bag
5. links
6. necklace

WORKBOOK PAGE 73

A. WHAT'S THE WORD?

1. tight
3. small
5. light
2. loose
4. large
6. heavy

7. short
9. striped
11. low
8. long
10. polka-dot
12. high

B. MATCHING: OPPOSITES

1. short
2. light
3. baggy
4. plain
5. narrow

WORKBOOK PAGE 74

A. WHICH DEPARTMENT?

1. Furniture
2. Jewelry
3. Men's Clothing
4. Household Appliances
5. Housewares
6. Women's Clothing
7. Electronics

B. MATCHING

1. bar
2. room
3. garage
4. fountain
5. department

WORKBOOK PAGE 75

A. WHAT'S THE WORD?

a. TV
b. camcorder
c. VCR
d. speaker
e. stereo system
f. CD player
g. tape recorder
h. radio

B. MATCHING

1. recorder
2. radio
3. camera
4. player
5. control

WORKBOOK PAGE 76

A. WHAT'S THE WORD?

a. computer
b. monitor
c. keyboard
d. mouse
e. printer
f. telephone
g. calculator
h. camera

B. WHICH GROUP?

For a camera:	For a computer:
film	keyboard
camera case	modem
tripod	mouse
zoom lens	printer

WORKBOOK PAGE 77

A. WHAT'S THE WORD?

a. blocks
b. toy truck
c. doll
d. doll house
e. crayons
f. coloring book
g. wagon
h. swing set
i. bicycle
j. jump rope
k. tricycle
l. skateboard

WORKBOOK PAGES 78–79

A. WHAT IS IT?

1. nickel
2. penny
3. quarter
4. half dollar
5. dime
6. dollar bill

B. WHAT'S THE VALUE?

1. 10¢
2. 1¢
3. 5¢
4. $1.00
5. 25¢
6. 50¢

C. MATCHING

1. $.10
2. $10.00
3. $.50
4. $1.00
5. $.01

D. WHAT'S THE AMOUNT?

1. $.05
2. $.15
3. $.30
4. $.12
5. $.26
6. $.25
7. $.75
8. $15.00

E. LISTENING

Listen and circle the amount you hear.

1. A. How much is this?
   B. Twenty-five cents.
   A. Twenty-five cents?
   B. Yes.
2. A. How much is this?
   B. Ten dollars.
   A. Ten dollars?
   B. Yes.
3. A. How much is this?
   B. Forty-four cents.
   A. Forty-four cents?
   B. Yes.
4. A. How much is this?
   B. Sixty-one dollars.
   A. Sixty-one dollars?
   B. Yes.
5. A. How much is this?
   B. Seven dollars and ten cents.
   A. Seven dollars and ten cents?
   B. Yes.
6. A. How much is this?
   B. Forty-one dollars and fourteen cents.
   A. Forty-one dollars and fourteen cents?
   B. Yes.

Answers

1. $.25
2. $10.00
3. $.44
4. $61.00
5. $7.10
6. $41.14

WORKBOOK PAGES 80–81

A. CHOOSE THE CORRECT WORD

1. check
2. credit card
3. money order
4. deposit slip
5. bank book
6. traveler's check

C. AT THE BANK

(Students should write correct date, account number, and amount on each bank slip. They should also put their signature on #1 and #2.)

WORKBOOK PAGES 82–83

A. WHAT IS IT?

a. head
b. hair
c. eye
d. ear
e. nose
f. mouth
g. teeth
h. chin
i. neck
j. shoulder
k. chest
l. back
m. arm
n. elbow
o. waist
p. leg

B. WHAT IS IT?

a. hand
b. finger
c. thumb
d. foot
e. ankle
f. toe

C. MATCHING: WHERE ARE THEY?

1. neck
2. hand
3. foot
4. mouth
5. head
6. arm

D. HOW MANY DO WE HAVE?

1. 2
2. 10
3. 1
4. 2
5. 1
6. 10
7. 1
8. 2
9. 1
10. 2

WORKBOOK PAGES 84–86

A. CHOOSE THE CORRECT WORD

1. insect bite
2. headache
3. stomachache
4. fever
5. cough
6. toothache
7. cold
8. stiff neck
9. the chills

B. LISTENING

Listen and circle the word you hear.

1. A. What's the matter?
   B. I have a headache.
   A. A headache? I'm sorry to hear that.
2. A. What's the matter?
   B. I have a cold.
   A. A cold? I'm sorry to hear that.
3. A. What's the matter?
   B. I have a stomachache.
   A. A stomachache? I'm sorry to hear that.
4. A. What's the matter?
   B. I have a virus.
   A. A virus? I'm sorry to hear that.
5. A. What's the matter?
   B. I have a fever.
   A. A fever? I'm sorry to hear that.
6. A. What's the matter?
   B. I have the hiccups.
   A. The hiccups? I'm sorry to hear that.

Answers

1. headache
2. cold
3. stomachache
4. virus
5. fever
6. hiccups

C. CHOOSE THE CORRECT WORD

1. dizzy
2. burn
3. cut
4. exhausted
5. cough

D. WORDSEARCH (see p. 155)

E. CROSSWORD (see p. 155)

WORKBOOK PAGE 87

A. CHOOSE THE CORRECT WORD

1. dentist
2. pediatrician
3. X-ray technician
4. surgeon
5. optometrist
6. EMT
7. stethoscope
8. thermometer
9. scale

B. MATCHING

1. lab technician
2. dentist
3. optometrist
4. cardiologist
5. pediatrician

WORKBOOK PAGE 88

A. CHOOSE THE CORRECT WORD

1. sling
2. injection
3. cast
4. exercise
5. surgery
6. stitches
7. I.V.
8. hospital bed
9. bandaid

B. MATCHING

1. therapy
2. tests
3. button
4. pan
5. gown

WORKBOOK PAGE 89

A. CHOOSE THE CORRECT WORD

1. eye drops
2. aspirin
3. antacid tablets
4. vitamins
5. heating pad
6. cold tablets
7. capsule
8. pill
9. teaspoon

B. MATCHING

1. syrup
2. lozenges
3. spray
4. pad
5. tablets

WORKBOOK PAGE 90

A. WHAT'S THE WORD?

1. envelope
2. stamp
3. postcard
4. letter
5. package
6. mailbox
7. zip code
8. air letter
9. money order

B. MATCHING

1. carrier
2. address
3. mail
4. order
5. post
6. code

WORKBOOK PAGE 91

A. WHAT'S THE WORD?

1. librarian
2. checkout desk
3. shelves
4. card catalog
5. atlas
6. encyclopedia
7. newspaper
8. magazine

B. WHICH SECTION OF THE LIBRARY?

Reference:	Periodicals:	Media:
dictionary	newspaper	videotape
encyclopedia	magazine	tape

WORKBOOK PAGE 92

A. WHERE ARE THEY?

1. principal, office
2. coach, gym
3. custodian, cafeteria
4. nurse, nurse's office
5. guidance counselor, guidance office
6. teacher, chemistry lab

WORKBOOK PAGE 93

A. WHAT'S THE WORD?

1. health
2. history
3. French
4. band
5. science
6. math
7. art
8. music
9. football

B. WHICH GROUP?

Languages:	Math:	Science:
French	algebra	biology
Spanish	geometry	chemistry

WORKBOOK PAGES 94–95

A. WHAT'S THE OCCUPATION?
1. butcher
2. assembler
3. cashier
4. farmer
5. chef
6. barber
7. courier
8. baker
9. accountant
10. custodian
11. architect
12. firefighter

B. MATCHING: THE SAME JOB
1. reporter
2. custodian
3. chef
4. messenger
5. bricklayer

C. MATCHING: WHO USES IT?
1. accountant
2. custodian
3. carpenter
4. chef
5. artist
6. cashier
7. gardener
8. barber

WORKBOOK PAGES 96–97

A. WHAT'S THE OCCUPATION?
1. pharmacist
2. plumber
3. salesperson
4. mechanic
5. teacher
6. welder
7. secretary
8. painter
9. scientist
10. waiter
11. waitress
12. lawyer

B. MATCHING: WHO WORKS THERE?
1. mechanic
2. secretary
3. teacher
4. waiter
5. salesperson
6. pharmacist

C. CROSSWORD (see p. 155)

WORKBOOK PAGES 98–99

A. WHAT DO THEY DO?
1. paint
2. cook
3. serve
4. sell
5. clean
6. wash
7. deliver
8. drive
9. type
10. file
11. sew
12. assemble

B. MATCHING
1. bake.
2. act.
3. drive.
4. paint.
5. assemble components.
6. build things.
7. clean.

C. MATCHING
1. buildings.
2. food.
3. lawns.
4. an airplane.
5. the piano.
6. cars.

WORKBOOK PAGE 100

A. WHAT'S THE WORD?
a. coat rack
b. message board
c. copier
d. typist
e. file cabinet
f. file clerk
g. coffee machine
h. water cooler

B. MATCHING
1. board
2. cooler
3. cabinet
4. lounge
5. machine

WORKBOOK PAGE 101

A. CHOOSE THE CORRECT WORD
1. telephone
2. computer
3. printer
4. calculator
5. postal scale
6. paper cutter

B. LISTENING
Listen. Write the correct number.
1. (Sound: telephone)
2. (Sound: electric pencil sharpener)
3. (Sound: adding machine)
4. (Sound: typewriter)
5. (Sound: fax machine)
6. (Sound: printer)

Answers

2	1
4	3
5	6

WORKBOOK PAGE 102

A. WHAT IS IT?
1. pen
2. desk
3. clipboard
4. pencil
5. eraser
6. wastebasket
7. scissors
8. stapler
9. file cabinet

B. MATCHING
1. calendar
2. cabinet
3. stamp
4. chair
5. dispenser
6. opener

WORKBOOK PAGE 103

A. CHOOSE THE CORRECT WORD
1. envelope
2. glue
3. paper clip
4. staple
5. index card
6. file folder
7. rubber band
8. thumbtack
9. gluestick

B. MATCHING
1. tape
2. paper
3. clip
4. band
5. card

WORKBOOK PAGE 104

A. CHOOSE THE CORRECT WORD
1. time clock
2. first-aid kit
3. cafeteria
4. forklift
5. conveyor belt
6. assembly line
7. safety glasses
8. hand truck
9. suggestion box

B. MATCHING
1. clock
2. line
3. station
4. kit
5. belt

WORKBOOK PAGE 105

A. WHAT'S THE WORD?
1. helmet
2. ladder
3. bulldozer
4. cement
5. wire
6. dump truck
7. wood
8. brick
9. wheelbarrow

B. WHICH GROUP?

Materials:
beam
pipe
plywood

Machines:
backhoe
bulldozer
cement mixer

WORKBOOK PAGES 106–107

A. WHAT'S THE WORD?

1. battery
2. engine
3. radiator
4. tire
5. headlight
6. bumper

7. gas station
8. gas pump
9. mechanic
10. flare
11. jack
12. spare tire

B. MATCHING

1. wipers
2. defroster
3. plate
4. plugs
5. belt

C. CHOOSE THE CORRECT WORD

1. seat belt
2. steering wheel
3. accelerator
4. gearshift
5. gas gauge
6. rearview mirror
7. radio
8. sedan
9. minivan

D. MATCHING

1. bag
2. belt
3. mirror
4. signal
5. brake

WORKBOOK PAGE 108

A. WHAT'S THE WORD?

1. tollbooth
2. tunnel
3. crosswalk
4. stop sign
5. bridge
6. traffic light
7. school crossing
8. railroad crossing

B. LISTENING

Listen. Write the number under the correct sign.

1. A. The sign says No Right Turn.
   B. No Right Turn?
   A. Yes.
2. A. The sign says Do Not Enter.
   B. Do Not Enter?
   A. Yes.
3. A. The sign says No Left Turn.
   B. No Left Turn?
   A. Yes.
4. A. The sign says Stop.
   B. Stop?
   A. Yes.
5. A. The sign says No U Turn.
   B. No U Turn?
   A. Yes.

Answers

3   1   4   5   2

WORKBOOK PAGE 109

A. WHAT'S THE WORD?

1. bus
2. taxi
3. bus station
4. conductor
5. luggage
6. train
7. bus driver
8. bus stop
9. subway

B. MATCHING

1. car
2. driver
3. compartment
4. booth
5. station

WORKBOOK PAGE 110

A. CHOOSE THE CORRECT WORD

1. suitcase
2. ticket
3. customs officer
4. passport
5. security guard
6. boarding pass
7. baggage claim area
8. metal detector

B. MATCHING

1. officer
2. guard
3. counter
4. pass
5. detector

WORKBOOK PAGE 111

A. CHOOSE THE CORRECT WORD

1. meal
2. pilot
3. lavatory
4. life vest
5. helicopter
6. seat belt

B. MATCHING

1. exit
2. belt
3. bag
4. attendant
5. compartment
6. seat
7. sign

WORKBOOK PAGE 112

A. CROSSWORD (see p. 156)

WORKBOOK PAGE 113

A. CHOOSE THE CORRECT WORD

1. tent
2. lantern
3. compass
4. sleeping bag
5. backpack
6. thermos

B. WHAT'S THE WORD?

1. bag
2. hiking
3. tent
4. picnic
5. rock
6. map

C. MATCHING

1. stove
2. map
3. bag
4. boots
5. basket

WORKBOOK PAGE 114

A. WHAT'S THE WORD?

1. seesaw
2. bench
3. rest rooms
4. grill
5. zoo
6. sandbox
7. trash can
8. slide
9. swings

B. MATCHING

1. table
2. can
3. rooms
4. fountain
5. rack

WORKBOOK PAGE 115

A. CHOOSE THE CORRECT WORD

1. shovel
2. kite
3. snack bar
4. surfer
5. bathing cap
6. lifeguard
7. surfboard
8. cooler
9. seashell

B. MATCHING

1. ball
2. lotion
3. suit
4. preserver
5. bar

WORKBOOK PAGE 116

A. CROSSWORD (see p. 156)

B. MATCHING

1. shorts
2. pong
3. out
4. riding
5. skating

WORKBOOK PAGE 117

A. WHAT'S THE SPORT?

1. football
2. ice hockey
3. baseball
4. soccer
5. lacrosse
6. basketball

B. WHICH GROUP?

field:	rink:	court:
soccer	ice hockey	basketball
softball		volleyball

WORKBOOK PAGE 118

A. WHAT'S THE WORD?

1. volleyball
2. volleyball net
3. basketball
4. backboard
5. baseball
6. bat
7. hockey puck
8. hockey stick

B. LISTENING

Listen. Write the number next to the correct picture.

1. A. I can't find my football helmet.
   B. Your football helmet? Look in the closet.
2. A. I can't find my lacrosse stick.
   B. Your lacrosse stick? Look in the closet.
3. A. Excuse me. I'm looking for a basketball.
   B. Our basketballs are over there.
   A. Thanks.
4. A. Excuse me. I'm looking for a baseball bat.
   B. Our baseball bats are over there.
   A. Thanks.
5. A. I'm going to play hockey after school today.
   B. Don't forget your hockey mask.
6. A. I'm going to play soccer after school today.
   B. Don't forget your shinguards.

Answers

| 3 | 6 | 1 |
| 2 | 4 | 5 |

WORKBOOK PAGE 119

A. CHOOSE THE CORRECT WORD

1. ice skates
2. sled
3. toboggan
4. snowmobiling
5. bobsled
6. poles
7. cross-country skiing

B. MATCHING

1. guards
2. skates
3. dish
4. skiing
5. boots

WORKBOOK PAGE 120

A. WHAT'S THE WORD?

1. swimming
2. fishing
3. sailing
4. surfing
5. rafting
6. waterskiing
7. canoeing
8. kayaking
9. snorkeling

B. MATCHING

1. snorkeling
2. fishing
3. rowing
4. canoeing
5. swimming
6. surfing

WORKBOOK PAGE 121

A. CHOOSE THE CORRECT WORD

1. reach
2. sit
3. kick
4. hit
5. bounce
6. lift
7. dive
8. serve
9. sit-up
10. leg lift
11. deep knee bend

B. LISTENING

Listen. Write the number under the correct picture.

1. A. Pitch the ball!
   B. Pitch the ball? Okay, Coach!
2. A. Now do a handstand!
   B. A handstand?
   A. Yes.
3. A. Now do a somersault!
   B. A somersault?
   A. Yes.
4. A. Dribble the ball!
   B. Dribble the ball? Okay, Coach.
5. A. Okay, everybody. I want you to do twenty push-ups!
   B. Twenty push-ups?!
   A. That's right.
6. A. Okay, everybody. I want you to do thirty jumping jacks!
   B. Thirty jumping jacks?!
   A. That's right.

Answers

| 2 | 5 | 4 | 6 | 1 | 3 |

WORKBOOK PAGE 122

A. CHOOSE THE CORRECT WORD
1. checkers
2. marbles
3. thread
4. astronomy
5. pottery
6. stamp album
7. sculpture
8. binoculars
9. sewing machine

B. MATCHING
1. weaving
2. sewing
3. pottery
4. photography
5. astronomy

WORKBOOK PAGE 123

A. WHAT'S THE WORD?
1. conductor
2. musician
3. actor
4. actress
5. ballerina
6. toeshoes
7. lobby
8. screen

B. MATCHING
1. office
2. dancer
3. screen
4. stand
5. orchestra

WORKBOOK PAGE 124

A. CHOOSE THE CORRECT WORD
1. rock music
2. musical
3. comedy
4. jazz
5. cartoon
6. game show

B. LISTENING
Listen. Write the number next to the type of music you hear.
1. (Sound: rap music)
2. (Sound: country)
3. (Sound: jazz)
4. (Sound: classical)
5. (Sound: rock)
6. (Sound: gospel)
7. (Sound: reggae)

Answers

4	3	7	1
6	2	5	

WORKBOOK PAGE 125

A. CHOOSE THE CORRECT WORD
1. violin
2. drum
3. piano
4. guitar
5. trumpet
6. clarinet

B. WHICH GROUP?

Brass:	Strings:	Woodwinds:
trombone	cello	clarinet
trumpet	violin	flute

C. LISTENING
Listen. Write the number next to the instrument you hear.
1. (Sound: harmonica)
2. (Sound: flute)
3. (Sound: banjo)
4. (Sound: tuba)
5. (Sound: harp)
6. (Sound: drum)

Answers

4	6	2
1	5	3

WORKBOOK PAGE 126

A. CHOOSE THE CORRECT WORD
1. flower
2. cone
3. trunk
4. tulip
5. bush
6. cactus

B. WHAT'S MISSING?
1. tree
2. dogwood
3. plant
4. daffodil
5. grass
6. flower

C. WHICH GROUP?

flowers:	trees:
rose	palm
daisy	pine
tulip	maple
sunflower	oak

WORKBOOK PAGE 127

A. CHOOSE THE CORRECT WORD
1. river
2. desert
3. forest
4. dam
5. waterfall
6. field

B. WHAT'S MISSING?
1. lake
2. pond
3. cliff
4. river
5. jungle
6. ocean

C. MATCHING
1. pollution
2. waste
3. gas
4. energy
5. rain

WORKBOOK PAGE 128

A. WHAT'S THE WORD?
1. field
2. tractor
3. scarecrow
4. barn
5. silo
6. hay
7. farmer
8. cow
9. rooster

B. MATCHING
1. lamb
2. calf
3. chick
4. kid
5. piglet

C. LISTENING

Listen. Write the number next to the farm animal you hear.

1. (Sound: turkey)
2. (Sound: chick)
3. (Sound: cow)
4. (Sound: goat)
5. (Sound: horse)
6. (Sound: lamb)
7. (Sound: pig)
8. (Sound: rooster)

Answers

5	2	7	1
6	8	3	4

WORKBOOK PAGE 129

A. WHAT'S THE WORD?

1. rabbit
2. deer
3. monkey
4. lion
5. horse
6. cat
7. elephant
8. dog
9. camel
10. squirrel
11. mouse
12. skunk

B. LISTENING

Listen. Write the number next to the animal or pet you hear.

1. (Sound: lion)
2. (Sound: bear)
3. (Sound: mouse)
4. (Sound: hyena)
5. (Sound: donkey)
6. (Sound: dog)
7. (Sound: cat)
8. (Sound: elephant)

Answers

5	2	6	4
3	7	1	8

WORKBOOK PAGE 130

A. WHAT'S THE WORD?

1. robin
2. fly
3. moth
4. owl
5. spider
6. ant
7. eagle
8. parrot

B. WHICH GROUP?

Insects:		Birds:	
bee	termite	swan	goose
beetle	mosquito	crow	pigeon

C. LISTENING

Listen. Write the number next to the bird or insect you hear.

1. (Sound: cricket)
2. (Sound: crow)
3. (Sound: duck)
4. (Sound: owl)
5. (Sound: bee)
6. (Sound: parrot)
7. (Sound: seagull)
8. (Sound: woodpecker)

Answers

3	4	6	2
7	5	1	8

WORKBOOK PAGE 131

A. WHAT'S THE WORD?

1. turtle
2. seal
3. frog
4. shrimp
5. whale
6. alligator
7. crab
8. dolphin
9. snake

B. MATCHING

1. walrus
2. tortoise
3. seal
4. lobster
5. octopus

WORKBOOK PAGES 132–133

A. WHAT'S THE WORD?

1. circle
2. rectangle
3. triangle
4. line
5. square
6. cone
7. cube
8. cylinder
9. pyramid
10. angle
11. sphere
12. ellipse

B. WHICH GROUP?

triangle:	circle:	rectangle:
base	radius	width
hypotenuse	diameter	length

C. WHAT'S THE WORD?

a. inch
b. foot
c. yard
d. centimeter
e. meter

D. MATCHING

1. centimeter
2. meter
3. mile
4. kilometer
5. inch
6. foot
7. yard

E. WHAT'S THE ANSWER?

1. 1
2. 12
3. yd. (yard)
4. mi. (mile)
5. 3
6. 1

WORKBOOK PAGE 134

A. WHAT'S THE WORD?

1. rocket
2. moon
3. sun
4. satellite
5. star
6. comet
7. Earth
8. astronaut

B. WHAT'S MISSING?

1. Mars
2. Pluto
3. Venus
4. Jupiter
5. Neptune
6. Mercury

C. MATCHING

1. shuttle
2. rocket
3. pad
4. eclipse
5. control

WORKBOOK PAGE 49

C. WORDSEARCH

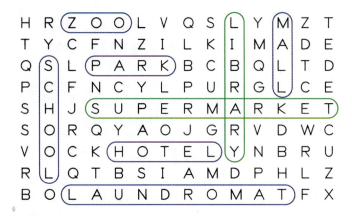

WORKBOOK PAGE 63

C. WORDSEARCH

WORKBOOK PAGE 68

B. CROSSWORD

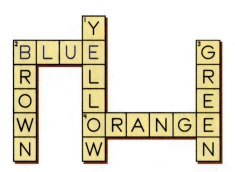

WORKBOOK PAGE 85

D. WORDSEARCH

```
V  F  D  H  R  B  M  P  C  D  I  E  G  H
Q  D  I  V  E  R  M  D  O  O  R  M  S  F
C  Q  Z  I  S  L  F  W  L  P  G  N  N  E
U  L  Z  U  V  H  E  A  D  A  C  H  E  V
A  U  Y  R  A  C  V  L  I  Q  H  U  E  E
T  E  R  W  A  P  E  E  P  A  S  D  Z  W
P  S  U  N  B  U  R  N  O  G  R  C  E  Q
Z  F  N  O  P  W  R  G  S  Q  E  X  H  B
```

WORKBOOK PAGE 86

E. CROSSWORD

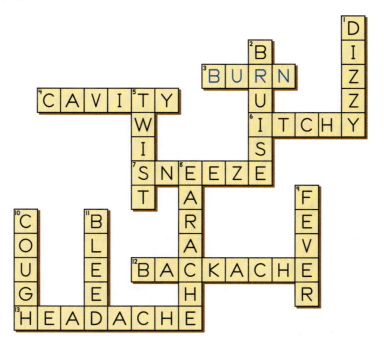

WORKBOOK PAGE 97

C. CROSSWORD

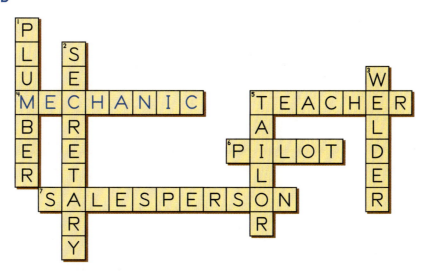

WORKBOOK PAGE 112

A. CROSSWORD

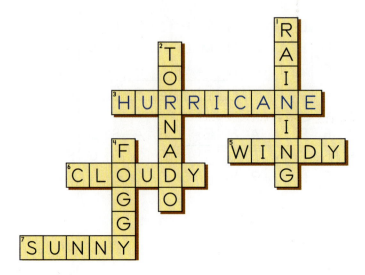

WORKBOOK PAGE 116

A. CROSSWORD

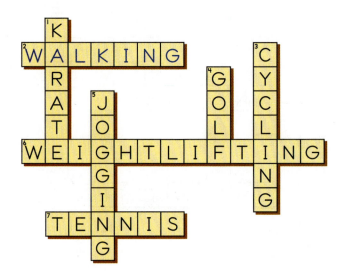